Practice **Book**

☐ NATIONAL GEOGRAPHIC
Reach
for Reading

COMMON CORE PROGRAM

 **NATIONAL
GEOGRAPHIC**

 Hampton-Brown

Acknowledgments

Grateful acknowledgment is given to the authors, artists, photographers, museums, publishers, and agents for permission to reprint copyrighted material. Every effort has been made to secure the appropriate permission. If any omissions have been made or if corrections are required, please contact the Publisher.

Cover Design and Art Direction: Visual Asylum

Cover Illustration: Joel Sotelo

Illustration Credits: All PM illustrations by National Geographic Learning.

Photographic Credits: PM1.28 FPG/Getty Images; PM1.29, PM1.30 Bettmann/Corbis; PM2.1 Amenhotepov/Shutterstock; PM2.30 Jason/Alamy; PM3.14 ROY TOFT/National Geographic Stock; PM3.15 PAUL NICKLEN/National Geographic Stock; PM3.30 ARMIN MAYWALD/FOTO NATURA/MINDEN PICTURES/National Geographic Stock; PM4.14 MPI/Getty Images; PM5.13 Michael P. Gadomski/Photo Researchers, Inc.; PM5.14 Marvin Dembinsky Photo Associates/Alamy; PM6.13, PM6.14, PM6.16 Bettmann/CORBIS; PM6.29 Doug Steley A/Alamy; PM7.14 ASSOCIATED PRESS; PM8.14 Dave Hogan/Stringer/Getty Images Entertainment; PM8.15 D. Hurst/Alamy; PM8.31 Mike Goldwater/Alamy.

For permission to use material from this text or product, submit all requests online at www.cengage.com/permissions

Further permissions questions can be emailed to permissionrequest@cengage.com

Visit National Geographic Learning online at www.NGSP.com

Visit our corporate website at www.cengage.com

Printed in the USA.

Printer: RR Donnelley, Harrisonburg, VA

ISBN: 978-11338-99655

12 13 14 15 16 17 18 19 20 21

10 9 8 7 6 5 4 3 2 1

Contents

Contents, continued

Contents, continued

Unit 7: Talking About Trash

Unit 8: One Idea

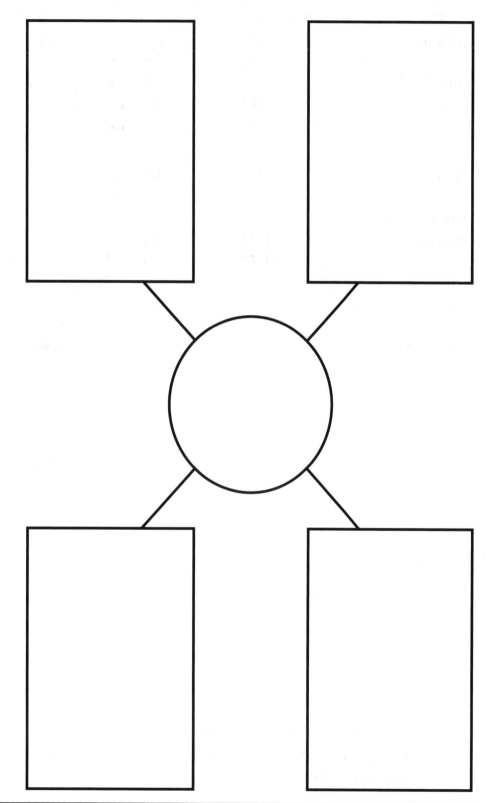

Unit Concept Map

Crossing Between Cultures

Make a concept map with the answers to the Big Question:
How can where you are change who you are?

Character Development Chart

How a Character Changes

Beginning	Middle	End
in the beginning amanda felt scared. These words prove that. am I the only one who is scared of leaving our home.	in the middle Of the story amanda felt a little bit happy. These wordsprove that. Today it feels good to laugh.	in the end amanda felt strong. these words prove that. papa was right. I am stronger than I thought. papa was right. I am stronger than I think--in mexico,in the states, any where.

 Use this chart to tell about a partner's favorite story. How does the character feel at first? How do the character's feelings change?

PM1.2

Grammar: Game

Simple Subjects and Predicates

With your partner, take turns choosing and circling the letter above the simple subject in the first part of the sentence and the letter above the simple predicate in the second part of the sentence. Then write the correct letters below to uncover a hidden question.

  a b c d e   f   g   h i
1. The kids in my class | love hamburgers and tacos.

  a b   c   d e f g h i j   k
2. My new neighbor | taught me how to do a Greek dance.

  a b c d   e   f   g   h
3. My friends at school | speak Spanish and English.

    a   b c   d   e f   g   h i j
4. Hundreds of people | attended the Swedish Festival in the park.

  a b c d   e f g h i   j   k
5. Last night my family | ate dinner at a Middle Eastern restaurant.

  a b c   d   e f g h   i   j   k
6. Juan, my older brother, | sings in a mariachi band every weekend.

__ ee __, __ o __, and __ r __ __ __ — __o th__y m__k__ lunch?

Grammar: Grammar and Writing

Edit and Proofread

Use the Editing and Proofreading Marks to correct the passage.
Look for correct usage of complete sentences.

Editing and Proofreading Marks

∧	Add.
℘	Take out.
/	Make lowercase.
∧ (with dot)	Add comma.
⊙	Add period.

My Aunt María ℘Grew up in Chicago, but her dad was born in Mexico. Every summer the whole family. Traveled back to his home village. For two days the traveled south, down through Missouri, Oklahoma, and Texas, and then over the border into Mexico. To me, it like fun. My did not like it. missed her friends in Chicago. Also, she never got to play sports in the summer or go to camp.

Today, Aunt María glad about their trips to Mexico every year. learned about her Mexican culture. Her grandmother in Mexico her how to make tamales and weave colorful rugs. Best of all, learned to speak Spanish as well as her dad!

Know the Test Format

Read the question about "My Diary from Here to There." Choose the best answer.

Sample

1 Who goes to the United States to get the green cards?

Ⓐ Mamá

Ⓑ Amada

● Papá

Ⓓ Victor

Read the question. Then write your answer on the lines provided.

2 Why does Michi say that Amada is lucky?

_____

_____

Read the prompt. Then write your answer on the lines provided.

3 Write a short paragraph to tell why crossing the border in Tijuana was a crazy experience for Amada's family.

_____

_____

_____

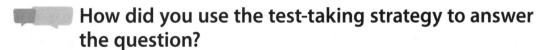 How did you use the test-taking strategy to answer the question?

_____

Name _____ Date _____

"My Diary from Here to There"

Beginning	Middle	End

 Use this chart to tell about Amada's story. Then use your character development chart to retell the story to a partner.

Fluency Practice

"My Diary from Here to There"

Expression in reading is how you use your voice to express feeling. Use this passage to practice reading with proper expression.

Today at breakfast, Mamá explained everything. She said, "Papá	9
lost his job. There's no work here, no jobs at all. We know moving will	24
be hard, but we want the best for all of you. Try to understand." I thought	40
the boys would be upset, but instead they got really excited about moving	53
to the States.	56
Am I the only one who is scared of leaving our home, our beautiful	70
country, and all the people we might never see again?	80

From "My Diary from Here to There" page 14

Expression

1 ☐ Does not read with feeling.

2 ☐ Reads with some feeling, but does not match content.

3 ☐ Reads with appropriate feeling for most content.

4 ☐ Reads with appropriate feeling for all content.

Accuracy and Rate Formula
Use the formula to measure a reader's accuracy and rate while reading aloud.

_____ − _____ = _____
words attempted   number of errors   words correct per minute
in one minute   (wcpm)

Name _____   Date _____

Looking at the Stars

Grammar Rules Sentences

Every sentence has a subject and a predicate.

- The **complete subject** includes all the words about the subject. The **simple subject** is the most important word in the subject.

- The **complete predicate** includes all the words that tell about the predicate. The **simple predicate** is the **verb**.

The eager young <u>student</u> studies the stars.

The stars <u>form</u> different shapes against the dark sky.

Read each sentence. Write the simple subject and the simple predicate.

1. Several of Misha's books have maps of the constellations.

   _____

2. The constellation maps show him what to look for in the sky.

   _____

3. Misha uses a telescope to get a closer look.

   _____

4. His favorite constellation so far is Scorpius.

   _____

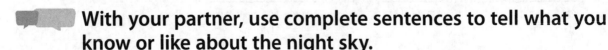 **With your partner, use complete sentences to tell what you know or like about the night sky.**

Grammar: Game

Phrases, Clauses, and Sentences, Oh My!

With a partner, take turns categorizing each word group as one type of clause or as a phrase.

1. Write each word group below under the correct heading in the chart.

2. For columns one and two, circle the subject and underline the verb in each word group.

- in a new land
- The journey lasted two months.
- because I lost my luggage
- before she learned English
- during the first year
- Grandpa told me about his life in his homeland.

Clause: Complete Sentence	Clause: Not a Complete Sentence	Phrase

Grammar: Game

Make a Sentence

Directions:

1. Copy each clause on a separate strip of paper. Put the strips face down in two sets—dependent clauses and independent clauses.

2. Take turns drawing a strip from each set. If you can, join the clauses into a sentence that makes sense, read the sentence aloud and score one point. Tell your partner where you would put a period and which letter should be capitalized.

3. If you cannot make a sentence, return one strip face down to the correct set and draw a replacement from that set.

4. Play until all the strips have been joined to form six sentences. The player with the most points wins.

Dependent Clauses	Independent Clauses
before my cousins left for the United States	my Dad and I met them at the airport
because there is so much to see and do here	they haven't seen their families for a year
since they came to America	everything seems strange
since they are new at school	we visit our cousins every week
when my cousins arrived	their friends gave them a going-away party
because we are good friends	they love their new country

Name _____ Date _____

Compare Genres

Compare fiction and nonfiction.

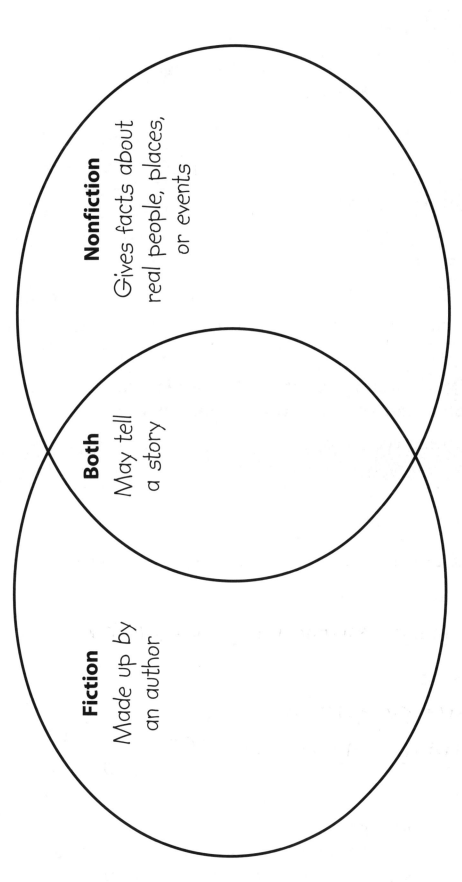

Nonfiction
Gives facts about real people, places, or events

Both
May tell a story

Fiction
Made up by an author

Take turns with a partner. Ask each other questions about the story and the oral history. Complete the diagram.

Name _____ Date _____

Grammar Rules Complete Sentences

1. A sentence must have a <u>subject</u> and a <u>predicate</u>.

   <u>His favorite grandmother</u> <u>makes good Korean food.</u>

2. The simple subject is what or whom the sentence is about: *grandmother*. The complete subject tells more about that subject: *His favorite grandmother*.

3. The simple predicate is the verb: *makes*. The complete predicate tells more about the predicate: *makes good Korean food*.

Read each group of words. Add a subject or a predicate to write a complete sentence. Use correct punctuation.

1. came to visit

She came to visit.

2. Greg's whole family

came over for dinner.

3. entered the harbor

They entered the harbor.

4. everyone on shore

Every one on shore wathea the whales go by.

Work with a partner. Pick one group of words from above. Think of as many complete sentences as you can and take turns saying them aloud to your partner.

Mark-Up Reading

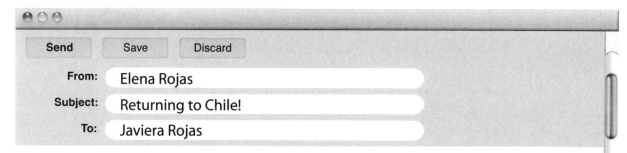

| Send | Save | Discard |

From: Elena Rojas

Subject: Returning to Chile!

To: Javiera Rojas

Dear Mamá,

We are thrilled that, after our long stay in the States, we are finally coming home to Chile. In just two days, we will all be together again! You can finally meet your infant granddaughter, Isabela! It has been years since her older sister Catalina was with you, and I know how eager she is to see her beloved grandparents again.

I am glad we have all had the opportunities to go to school in the United States, but our time here has not always been easy. Matias has had to work long hours at many jobs, and speaking English can still be a challenge sometimes. I am glad we have become bilingual, but it will be a relief to use Spanish again— as well as English!

The more I think about returning home, the more excited I get. I miss the ocean, my family, and the taste of cherimoya. You know it has always been my favorite fruit! Remember this picture I drew when I was Catalina's age? I even showed it to Catalina!

I have to go finish packing the last boxes, but I can't wait to see you on Friday!

Love,
Elena

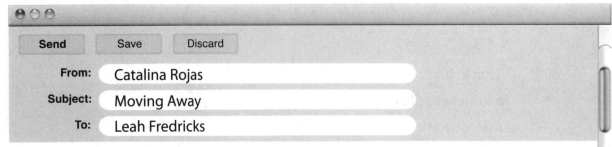

Mark-Up Reading

| Send | Save | Discard |

From: Catalina Rojas

Subject: Moving Away

To: Leah Fredricks

Mamá has been helping me pack up my things for our move to Chile. She is so excited to be going back to live there, but I am nervous and a little scared.

I'm going to miss you and everyone in our class a lot. It will be so weird to live in a quiet, tiny town instead of the busy, exciting city. What will we do there? Plus, the food will never be as good as your mom's delicious home-made pizza!

I'm also concerned about speaking Spanish. Will people understand me? At least my cousins will be at the same school and can help me.

I know that we will still e-mail each other, but I'm attaching a picture I drew of my family so you won't forget us.

Catalina

Explanation

Choose one e-mail. Explain how the narrator's viewpoint affects how she tells about the events. Give examples from the text.

_____

_____

_____

Grammar: Grammar and Writing

Edit and Proofread

Choose the Editing and Proofreading Marks you need to correct the passage. Look for correct usage of following:

- clauses and phrases
- subjects and predicates

Editing and Proofreading Marks

∧	Add.
♪	Take out.
/	Make lowercase.
∧	Add comma.
⊙	Add period.

We had a list of places that we wanted to see. When we visited New

York last spring. The Ellis Island Immigration Museum and the Statue

of Liberty at the top of our list. I was especially interested in visiting

these famous landmarks. Because we were studying them in school.

Early on the morning of our visit, we boarded a ferry in Battery

Park. in New York We could smell the salt spray as the ferry chugged

through the harbor to Liberty Island After we saw Lady Liberty. We

got back on the ferry and went to Ellis Island. Was really a thrill to see

the brick-and-limestone building loom up as we approached it. I'm

glad we got there early. Because there was so much to do and see in

the museum.

In El Salvador

Grammar Rules Clauses

A **clause** is a group of words that has a **subject** and **verb**.

- An **independent clause** is a complete sentence.

- A **dependent clause** does not express a complete thought. It is not a sentence.

A **dependent clause** can be combined with an **independent clause** to form a sentence.

El Salvador has a coastline.
<u>because the Pacific Ocean forms its southern border</u>

El Salvador has a coastline <u>because the Pacific Ocean forms its southern border</u>.

Read each item. Underline dependent clauses. If the sentence is incomplete, add words to complete it.

1. Because the forest in El Salvador is always wet and humid, it is a good habitat for orchids and ferns.

2. If you visit, you may see spider monkeys, porcupines, and toucans in the forest.

3. Many rivers which crocodiles and turtles depend on for survival

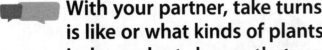 **With your partner, take turns describing what the U.S. is like or what kinds of plants or animals live here. Use independent clauses that express complete thoughts.**

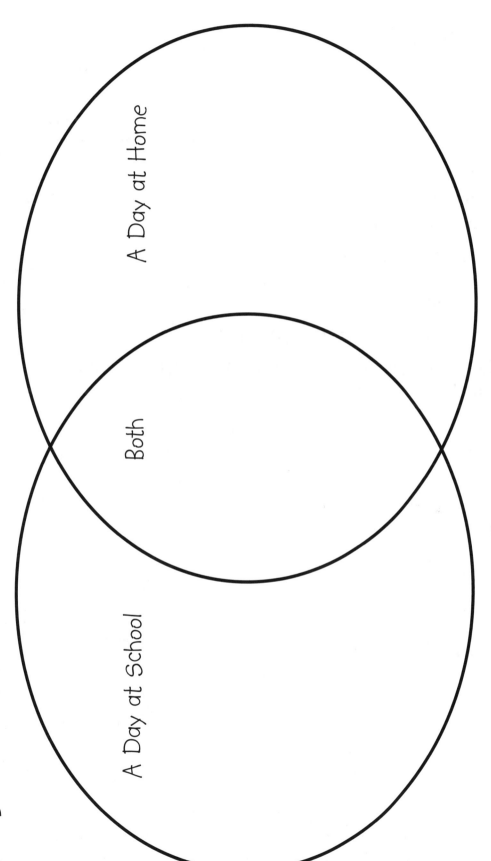

A Day at Home

Both

A Day at School

Use this diagram to compare and contrast a day at school with a day at home. Then talk with a partner about it.

Venn Diagram

Map and Talk

For use with TE p. T39a

PM1.17

Grammar: Game

No, Not, Nobody!

no	not	never	none
no one	nothing	nobody	nowhere

Directions:

1. Write one negative word from the box above in each space on the game board.

2. Take turns. Flip one coin, and use other coins as game markers. Move your marker forward two spaces for heads. Move back one space for tails.

3. Use the word you land on in a sentence.

4. The first player to land directly on "Finish" after circling the game board at least once wins.

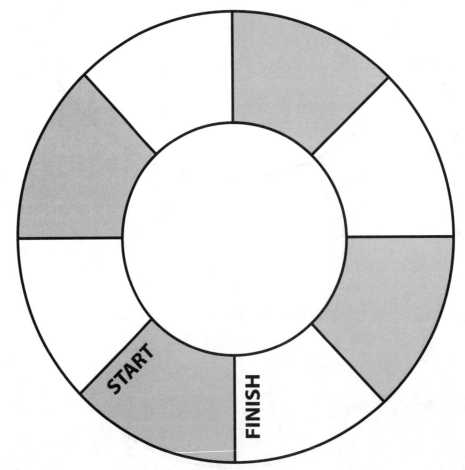

Grammar: Grammar and Writing

Edit and Proofread

Choose the Editing and Proofreading Marks you need to correct the passage. Look for correct usage of the following:

- negative sentences
- correlative conjunctions

Editing and Proofreading Marks

∧	Add.
ℒ	Take out.
⬭↗∧	Move to here.
∧̣	Add comma.
⊙	Add period.

Both Uncle Ahmed ~~or~~ *and* Aunt Demet are happy that they left their

homeland many years ago. Yet it was none an easy decision to make.

They love not only their homeland but the family members they left

behind. According to Aunt Demet, they did not have no choice. There

was neither economic opportunity or political stability in their country.

Today, my aunt and uncle are happy and successful. They not

only run a business and also volunteer in the community. They help

local organizations whether they are busy and not. They don't want

to be nowhere else, although they have no forgotten their origins.

They contact family members all the time, and they don't have no

hesitation about flying back home often.

Name _____ Date _____

Know the Test Format

Read the question and choose the best answer.

Sample

> **1** In the phrase "reminding me of my heritage," what does the word <u>heritage</u> mean?
>
> ● background
>
> Ⓑ family
>
> Ⓒ party
>
> Ⓓ relationship

Read the questions. Then write your answer in the space provided.

2 What happened to John Bul Dau when he was twelve years old that changed his life?

_____

_____

_____

3 At the end of his story, John Bul Dau writes, "They call me a Lost Boy, but let me assure you, I am not lost anymore." Write what you think John means by this statement.

_____

_____

_____

 Tell a partner how you used the strategy to answer the questions.

Name _____ Date _____

Venn Diagram

"A Refugee Remembers"

Use the diagram to tell a partner how life was the same for John Bul Dau in each place.

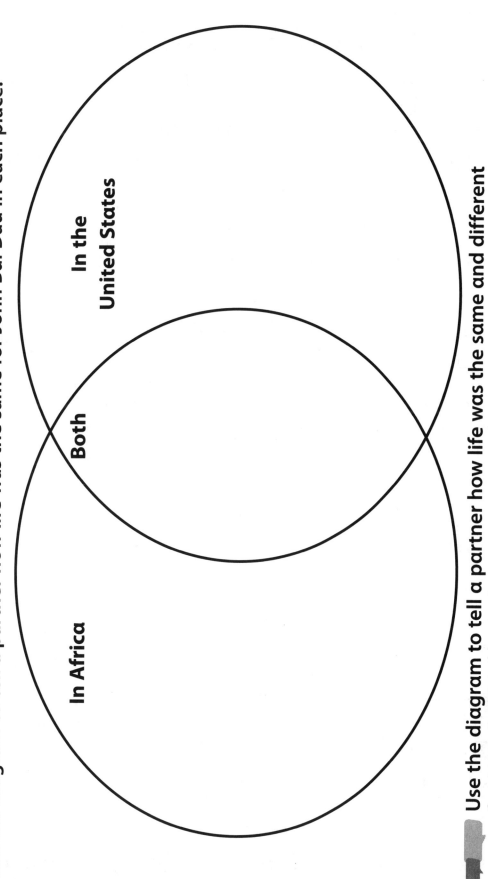

In the
United States

Both

In Africa

Use the diagram to tell a partner how life was the same and different for John Bul Dau in each place.

Fluency Practice

"A Refugee Remembers"

When you read with proper expression, you show feeling in your voice as you read. Use this passage from p. 49 to practice reading with expression. Look for words that tell you about the mood or feeling of what you are reading. Then match this feeling with your voice as you read.

All that night, as we waited in the grass for	10
death or daybreak, I thought the man who pulled me	20
to safety was my father. When the sun began to rise,	31
I learned I was wrong. Abraham Deng Niop was	40
my neighbor.	42
After about two hours the guns fell silent and we	52
heard no more sounds from the village. Abraham told	61
me we ought to move.	66
Every time we heard noises coming toward us,	74
we ducked into the forest or the tall grass. Soldiers kept	85
passing. When they disappeared, we started running again.	93
East seemed a good direction; we heard no guns as we	104
ran toward the rising sun.	109

Expression

1 ☐ Does not read with feeling.	**3** ☐ Reads with appropriate feeling for most content.
2 ☐ Reads with some feeling, but does not match content.	**4** ☐ Reads with appropriate feeling for all content.

Accuracy and Rate Formula
Use the formula to measure a reader's accuracy and rate while reading aloud.

_____	−	_____	=	_____
words attempted in one minute		number of errors		words correct per minute (wcpm)

Grammar: Reteach

The Soccer Game

Grammar Rules Sequences and Conjunctions

A **negative sentence** uses a **negative word** to say "no." Use one negative word in a sentence.	The soccer game yesterday was **not** boring.
Conjunctions connect words or groups of words. **Correlative conjunctions** are used in pairs.	Ian scored **not only** two goals **but also** two penalty kicks.

Add a negative word to turn each sentence into a negative sentence. Write the new sentence.

never	no one
nobody	not

1. The Bears scored against the Wildcats.

_____

2. Their goalee could stop the ball from getting past him.

_____

3. The players kicked goals.

_____

Choose conjunctions to complete each sentence.

either	or
not only	but also

4. _____ the Bears had a bad day, _____ they didn't practice enough.

5. _____ will their team caption ask what went wrong, _____ their coach will.

Describe a recent sports event to a partner. Did you use negative sentences or correlative conjunctions?

Grammar: Game

Sentence Spinner

Directions:

1. Take turns spinning the spinner.

2. Complete the sentence with a compound subject.

3. Play until you have completed all the sentences. Then play another round!

Make a Spinner
1. Push a brad through the center of the circle.
2. Open the brad in the back.
3. Hook a paper clip over the top of the brad to make a spinner.

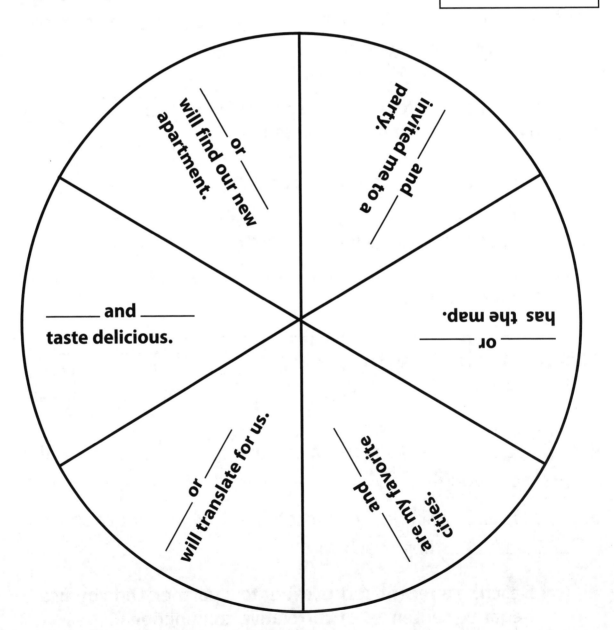

will find our new
apartment.
or
_____

_____ and _____
taste delicious.

or _____
will translate for us.

_____ and
are my favorite
cities.

_____ and _____
invited me to a
party.

or _____
has the map.

Grammar: Game

Connect the Verbs

1. Cut apart the word cards and spread them out face down.

2. Take turns. Turn over three cards. If you draw *and* or *or* with two verbs, make up a sentence with a compound predicate and keep your white verb cards.

3. If not, replace your cards.

4. Play until all the verb cards are gone. The player with the most cards wins.

and	or	hear	go
study	wait	travel	show
give	run	stand	work
open	see	learn	eat
talk	buy	find	meet

Name _____ Date _____

Compare Descriptive Language

John Bul Dau	Students in "American Stories"

 Take turns with a partner. Compare the descriptive language used in both selections.

Name _____ Date _____

Grammar Rules Compound Subjects

1. When **and** joins two simple subjects, use a verb that tells about more than one.

2. When **or** joins two subjects, use a verb that agrees with the simple subject closest to it.

Read each pair of sentences. Combine the subjects into a compound subject and write the new sentence. Be sure your subject agrees with the verb.

1. Mom goes to the city. Dad goes to the city.

_____

2. The train brings them downtown. The bus brings them downtown.

_____

3. The grocery store is open. The bakery is open.

_____

4. The vegetables are fresh. The bread is fresh.

_____

Make two sentences with the same subjects. Have your partner combine them into one sentence with a compound subject.

Name _____ Date _____

Journey to Gold Mountain

by Allison Chen

Imagine it is 1848 in southeastern China. You are a teenager listening wide-eyed to a tale spun by an American trader. Gold has been discovered in California. Gold fever grips the world! Tales of fabulous wealth attract many young people in China who make the long, difficult voyage across the Pacific to "Gold Mountain," their name for California.

▲ Chinese immigrants called California *Gam Saan*, or Gold Mountain.

Some immigrants faced their first challenges on their voyages, which they made aboard American or European ships. Everything on these foreign ships seemed strange to these travelers. If you had never even seen a steamship, imagine how its thudding engines might frighten you!

One immigrant, who traveled to the United States as a young man, later recalled that he was afraid to eat the "unusual" food served to the passengers. As a result, he was half-starved when he reached San Francisco.

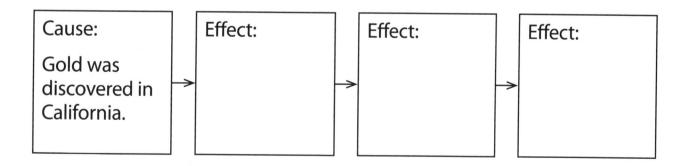

Cause: Gold was discovered in California.	→	Effect:	→	Effect:	→	Effect:

Journey to Gold Mountain (continued)

By the 1870s, hard times had fallen upon everyone across the nation. Millions of American workers lost their jobs and some people blamed the Chinese immigrants for high unemployment and low wages. American lawmakers responded by passing the Chinese Exclusion Act of 1882, which prevented almost all Chinese immigrants from entering the United States for ten years.

Soon, the American government had a problem on their hands. Floods of potential Chinese

▲ Chinese immigrants worked to build railroads.

immigrants were eager to enter the U.S., but the Chinese Exclusion Act made the immigration process long and difficult.

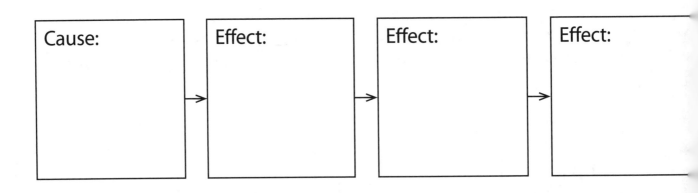

Cause:		Effect:		Effect:		Effect:
	→		→		→	

Mark-Up Reading

Journey to Gold Mountain (continued)

To provide housing for the immigrants, the government established the Angel Island Immigration Station in 1910 on a small island off the coast of San Francisco. Chinese immigrants were held at Angel Island for weeks or even years. Some expressed their bitterness and regret about the experience in poems that they carved into the wooden walls of their quarters. These verses, often called the "Gold Mountain" poems, became powerful statements of the strength of the immigrants' Chinese identity.

▲ Angel Island Immigration Station

Effect:	Effect:	Effect:	Effect:

Grammar: Grammar and Writing

Edit and Proofread

Choose the Editing and Proofreading Marks you need to correct the passage. Look for correct usage of the following:

- compound subjects and predicates
- subject-verb agreement

Editing and Proofreading Marks

∧	Add.
ℒ	Take out.
/	Make lowercase.
∧	Add comma.
⊙	Add period.

                    and
American football ∧ soccer are great sports, but I know many

Americans who don't follow soccer. Football or baseball get all their

attention. My American cousin and all his friends likes football the

best. They discuss their favorite teams know everything about the

players. During football season they watch each game on TV go to it.

They scream yell wherever they are.

I had to get used to that. Football games or football conversation

were the only thing around me. Then picture this scene. One day my

cousin and the guys asks me to a real game. The fans the big stadium

were exciting. Before I knew it, I was yelling, too! Now I follow football

and soccer. The Super Bowl and the World Cup is both important to me.

Name _____ Date _____

Did You Eat Your Vegetables?

Grammar Rules Subject and Predicates

A **compound subject** has two or more simple subjects joined by a <u>conjunction</u>. Use a plural verb when two subjects are joined by *and*. If the subjects are joined by *or*, look at the last subject. • If it is singular, use a singular verb. • If it is plural, use a plural verb.	Vegetables <u>and</u> fruits **are** good for you. These berries <u>or</u> this peach **tastes** sweet. This berry <u>or</u> these peaches **taste** sweet.
A **compound predicate** has two or more verbs joined by *and* or *or*.	People **bake** <u>or</u> **grill** vegetables.

Tell if the sentence has a compound subject or a compound predicate. For each sentence with a compound subject, draw an arrow to show which word(s) in the subject the verb agrees with.

1. Spinach and broccoli are healthy vegetables. _____

2. People boil or steam both of these foods. _____

3. An artichoke or carrots are healthy too. _____

4. A pad of butter or pinches of salt add to the flavor. _____

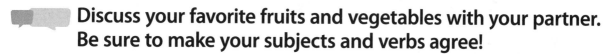 **Discuss your favorite fruits and vegetables with your partner. Be sure to make your subjects and verbs agree!**

     Unit 1 | Crossing Between Cultures

Catching the Light

Make a concept map with the answers to the Big Question:
What is the power of the sun?

Character Chart

Our Characters

Character	Role	Function	Conflict
Ri Jun	father	get the suns down	Sons want to ligth the sky all at once
ten suns	boys, 10 suns, suns	give Earth light	ignore Father mother to leave sky

What Else Am I Doing?

Directions:

1. Play with a partner to develop an imaginative story about an astronaut's trip to the sun.

2. Player 1 writes a simple sentence describing what the astronaut is doing.

3. Player 2 then spins the spinner and uses the participle on the wheel to write a participial phrase to add to the sentence.

4. Player 2 adds the participial phrase to the sentence and writes the new sentence on a separate piece of paper.

5. Switch roles and repeat for the next sentence. Players build on the earlier sentences to make a story.

6. Play until all the words on the spinner have been used.

7. Share your story with the class.

The astronaut climbed into the spaceship.

Dressed in his flight suit, the astronaut climbed into the spaceship.

Make a Spinner

1. Put a paper clip over the center of the spinner.
2. Touch the point of a pencil on the middle of the wheel and through the loop of the paper clip.
3. Spin the paper clip to make a spinner.

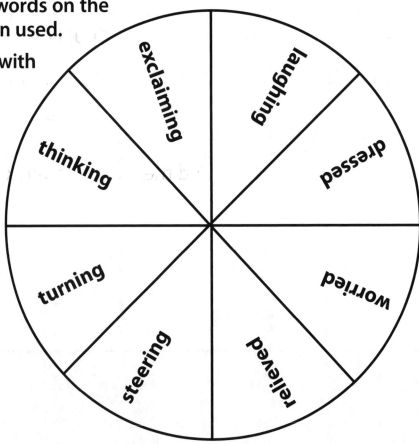

exclaiming · laughing · dressed · worried · relieved · steering · turning · thinking

Grammar: Grammar and Writing

Edit and Proofread

Choose the Editing and Proofreading Marks you need to correct the passage. Look for the following:

- correct use of introductory elements
- correct use of participial phrases
- correct use of commas

Editing and Proofreading Marks

∧	Add.
ℐ	Take out.
⌐‾‾⌐ ∧	Move to here.
∧	Add comma.
⊙	Add period.

Summer Discovery

On a bright summer day Quentin walked up to his front porch.

He saw a large pitcher of water tripping up the steps. In the pitcher

golden brown water had many tea bags floating in it. Quentin

feeling suspicious wondered why this pitcher was left on the porch.

Carefully Quentin carried the pitcher to the kitchen table.

Margaret saw the pitcher on the table walking into the kitchen.

Looked confused she asked Quentin why the sun tea was inside.

Cautiously Quentin asked Margaret what sun tea was. After a sip of

tea Quentin decided that he loved sun tea!

Test-Taking Strategy Practice

Read Directions Carefully

Answer the question by choosing the correct answer choice and shading the letter on your answer sheet.

Sample

1 What happened after Hu Yi shot the first arrow?

- Ⓐ New suns appeared.
- ● A sun shattered.
- Ⓒ Suns streaked higher.
- Ⓓ A sun circled Earth.

Read the question about "Ten Suns." Choose the best answer.

2 What did Hu Yi invent?

- Ⓐ the constellations
- Ⓑ the bow and arrow
- Ⓒ the ten suns
- Ⓓ the jade palace

Fill in the blank to complete the second sentence.

3 Di Jun's sons thought their job was _____ .

Read the question. Then write your answer in the space provided.

4 What did the emperor Shun tell his messenger?

_____

_____

_____

💬 **Tell a partner how you used the strategy to answer the questions.**

Name _____ Date _____

Character Chart

"Ten Suns"

Character	Role	Function	Conflict
Di Jun	father		sons want to light the sky all at once
ten sons			

Use your chart to retell the myth to a partner.

Fluency Practice

"Ten Suns"

Use this passage to practice reading with proper intonation.

Hu Yi refused. "How can I harm your boys? They are like my   13

children. I taught them to shoot with a bow and arrow. We both still   27

love them, even when they disobey."   33

"I love the creatures of Earth, too. I must protect them," Di Jun   46

told Hu Yi. "Do not be afraid. You will not harm the boys. My sons   61

will not be hurt, but they will be changed. Never again will they cross   75

the sky as suns. They will be gods no more. Hurry! Do as I command.   90

There is no time to spare. Earth is dying."   99

Intonation

1 ☐ Does not change pitch.

2 ☐ Changes pitch, but does not match content.

3 ☐ Changes pitch to match some of the content.

4 ☐ Changes pitch to match all of the content.

Accuracy and Rate Formula

Use the formula to measure a reader's accuracy and rate while reading aloud.

_____	−	_____	=	_____
words attempted in one minute		number of errors		words correct per minute (wcpm)

Name _____ Date _____

A Busy Day

Grammar Rules **Introductory Elements and Participial Phrases**	
An **introductory element** is a word, phrase, or clause that appears at the beginning of a sentence. It is always followed by a **comma**.	<u>Today</u>, we got up a 7 a.m. <u>Ten minutes later</u>, we took Max for walk.
Participles and **participial phrases** describe nouns or pronouns. They may appear before or after a noun, set off by **commas**. Always put a participial phrase next to the noun or pronoun it describes.	**Tugging on his leash**, Max started to run. The squirrel, **worried about the dog**, ran up a tree. **Chasing Max**, we got lots of exercise.

Underline the introductory elements. Circle the participial phrases. Add commas where they are needed.

1. Tired from the walk we thought about not going to the mall.

2. After resting a few minutes we decided to go.

3. At the mall we saw our friend Fran.

4. Fran, smiling and waving ran up to us.

5. Starved we all went to the food court for lunch.

 With your partner, describe something you did with a friend. Use introductory elements and participial phrases.

Grammar: Game

Depending on Clauses

Directions:

1. Play in a group of three to create sentences about the sun or about activities people enjoy in the sun.

2. Write each of the words below on a separate index card. Shuffle the cards and stack them face down.

3. Player 1 takes the top card and uses the word to write an introductory dependent clause. Then Player 1 places the word card at the bottom of the stack.

4. Player 2 completes the sentence by writing an independent clause that makes sense with the introductory clause. Remember to use a comma to separate the introductory clause from the rest of the sentence.

5. Player 3 acts as referee and awards one point each to Players 1 and 2 if their clauses are correct.

6. For the next turn, Player 2 draws a card and writes an introductory dependent clause. Shifting roles, Player 3 completes the sentence, and Player 1 acts as referee.

7. Continue changing roles and play until each player has been the referee twice. The player with the most points wins.

because	**while**	**until**	**although**
since	**if**	**when**	**before**

Grammar: Game

Change My Sentence

Types of Sentences		
direct address	yes/no answer	tag question

Directions:

1. Play in a group of three. Collaborate to write each type of sentence in the list on a separate index card. Then place the cards face down.

2. Player 1 chooses a card and sets it aside. He or she then writes a sentence about one of the characters in "Ten Suns" using the sentence type named on the card.

3. Players 2 and 3 are scorers. They read the sentence and decide if it is written correctly. They give Player 1 one point each for having the sentence in the correct form and for having the comma in the correct place.

4. Player 2 chooses one of the remaining cards and rewrites Player 1's original sentence using the sentence type labeled on the second card. Players 1 and 3 are scorers.

5. Play continues as Player 3 takes the last card and rewrites Player 1's original sentence using the third sentence type. Players 1 and 2 are scorers.

6. After Player 3's turn, reshuffle the cards and play another round with a new sentence, beginning with Player 2.

7. Continue playing until each player has started two sentences. The player with the most points at the end of the game wins.

Name _____   Date _____

Compare Origin Myths

	"Ten Suns"	"How the Fifth Sun Came to Be"
Tell the type of myth.		Aztec
Tell what the myth explains.		
Setting		Mexico
List the characters.	Gods: Heroes: Other:	Gods: Heroes: Other:
Tell what the story is about.	Beginning: Middle: End:	Beginning: Middle: End:
Tell the story's message.		

 Take turns with a partner. Share another message you think each myth has.

For use with TE p. T109a   **PM2.11**   **Unit 2** | Catching the Light

Grammar: Practice

The Story of the Sun

Grammar Rules Kinds of Sentences

1. Use a statement to tell something.
2. Use a command to tell someone to do something.
3. Use an exclamation to show strong feeling. End it with an exclamation mark. (!)
4. Use a question to ask something. End it with a question mark. (?)

Follow the directions. Use a contraction in at least one sentence.

1. **Write a statement about the sun's power.**

    _____

2. **Write an exclamation about the sun.**

    _____

3. **Write a question you have about the sun.**

    _____

4. **Write a command about staying safe in the sun.**

    _____

 Listen as a partner tells you something about the sun. Use a different kind of sentence to respond.

Mark-Up Reading

The **Sun God** and the **Moon God**

retold by Alonso Mantega

In the beginning of time, the people of the world lived in total darkness. There was no day, only endless night. The king of the birds, a vulture named Urubutsin, did not want light to reach the Earth below. So he commanded the birds to reflect the light back into the sky with their wings. By controlling the light, Urubutsin had power over the world. People struggled to survive in the dark and lived in fear.

▲ Urubutsin, a vulture, was king of the birds.

One day, two brothers named Kuat and Iae went out to gather food in the Amazon rainforest. Suddenly, a twig snapped behind the brothers.

"Who's there?" asked Kuat.

"*Grrrrrrraaar!*"

"A jaguar!" shouted Iae. "Run!"

The brothers sprinted back to their hut. "It is too dark," said Iae, collapsing into a hammock. "We cannot find food, and predators can stalk us!"

Kuat thought about how much he loved his home. But like all of the other people of the world, he found it difficult to survive in the darkness. This gave him an idea. "What we need is some of Urubutsin's light!" he said.

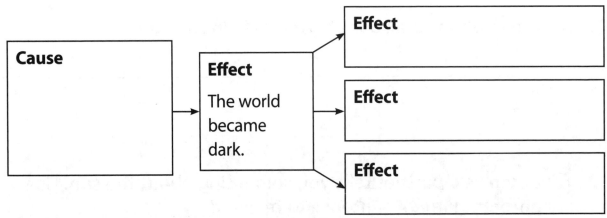

Cause	Effect	Effect
	The world became dark.	Effect
		Effect
		Effect

The **Sun God** and the **Moon God**   (continued)

The brothers decided to set a trap to capture Urubutsin. They knew that he loved to devour dead animals. Kuat found a jaguar carcass large enough to hide Iae and him. After they crawled inside, it was not long before Urubutsin saw the corpse. "Time to eat!" squealed the king of the birds as he swooped down on the carcass. But before he could tear into the meat, Kuat and Iae grabbed Urubutsin by the legs.

"Let me go!" squawked the king of the birds.

"Not until you give us some of your light!" replied Kuat.

"Never!" cawed the vulture as he struggled against the brothers' grips.

After hours and hours, Urubutsin was exhausted from trying to escape.

"Please," he chirped, "Let us compromise! I will let you have light for half of the day, and the other half will remain dark."

From that day forward, there was bright light during the day and even some light in the evening. The brothers became gods. Kuat, the caretaker of the daylight, was called the sun. Iae, who watched over the soft light at night, was the moon. Generations of their grateful tribesmen worshipped them for bringing light to a world that was once awash with darkness.

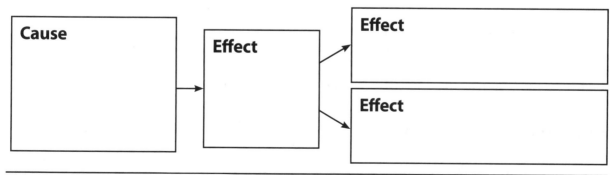

Grammar: Grammar and Writing

Edit and Proofread

Choose the Editing and Proofreading Marks you need to correct the passage. Look for the following:

- correct placement of commas
- correct use of introductory elements
- correct use of different sentence types

Editing and Proofreading Marks

∧	Add.
℘	Take out.
⊂⊃∧	Move to here.
⋀	Add comma.
⊙	Add period.

The Young Man and the Sun: An Island Legend

The young man had work to do, but the sun was setting. He couldn't work in the dark could he⸮If the sun moved more slowly he would have more time for his tasks. He asked his mother for help. "Mother I need a rope to catch the sun and make him slow down."

His mother said, "Yes I'll help. Cut some of my hair. Because it is strong it won't burn in the sun's heat." He made a long rope from her hair.

The next morning he threw the rope around the sun. The sun pleaded, "Young man release me won't you?" But the young man held fast.

He said, "Sun slow down so we can do our work!" The sun agreed. From that day on it moved more slowly for six months of the year.

Grammar: Reteach

What Do You Like to Read?

Grammar Rules Commas

Use **commas**:	
• after **introductory dependent clauses**	Although I like this story, I liked that, too.
• before or after the **name of someone being spoken to**	Tina, which one did you like? I liked the first one, Jacob.
• after a **yes or no answer**	Yes, I agree with you.
• before a **tag question** at the end of a statement	I like good stories, don't you?

Read each sentence. Add the missing commas and the correct end marks.

1. Antonio do you like historical fiction

2. Yes but I prefer science fiction stories Sam

3. Antonio look at the pictures in this book

4. Those are amazing Sam

5. After I read a good book I like to talk about it don't you

 With your partner, ask and answer *yes/no* questions about the stories you like. Use your partner's name in each sentence.

Goal-and-Outcome Chart

A School Project

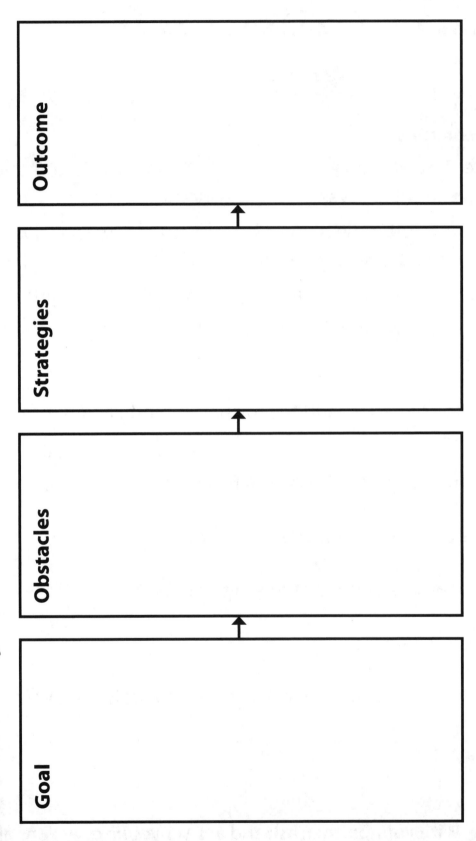

Goal

Obstacles

Strategies

Outcome

Use your chart to tell a partner about the goal and how it was achieved.

Grammar: Game

Electric Series!

Directions:

1. Play with a group of three or four players.

2. Cut out the cards and spread them out face up. Take turns selecting at least three white cards and one gray card.

3. Arrange your cards into a series of items. Place a paperclip between cards where commas should appear. You can use either form of the words that appear on the white cards.

4. If the other group members agree with your series, make up a sentence with the series and score one point. Then replace your cards. If they don't agree, replace your cards and the next player takes a turn.

5. Players who make a sensible sentence using a series of five or more white cards score an extra point.

6. Play until all players have had at least two turns. The player with the highest score wins.

and	or	battery batteries	shock shocks
spark sparks	light bulb light bulbs	television televisions	power cord power cords
plug plugs	switch switches	jolt jolts	lamp lamps
flashlight flashlights	burn burns	mobile device mobile devices	laptop laptops
outlet outlets	clock clocks	dial dials	power powers

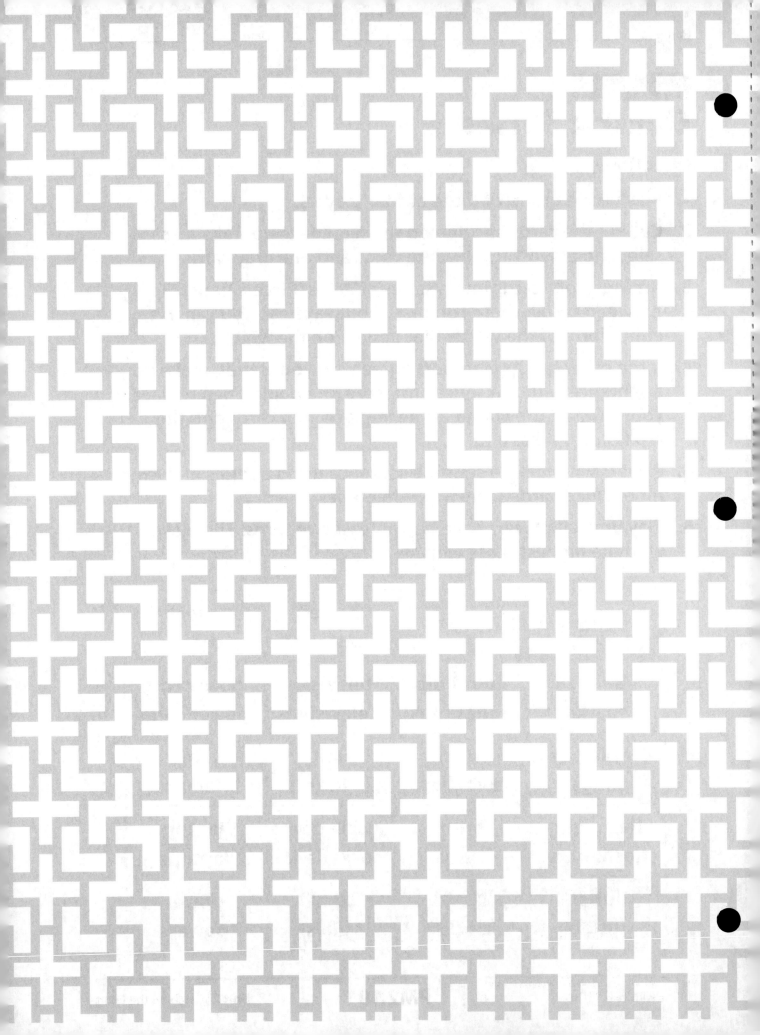

Grammar: Grammar and Writing

Edit and Proofread

Choose the Editing and Proofreading Marks you need to correct the passage. Look for the following:

- correct placement of commas and semicolons
- correct use of introductory elements
- correct use of different sentence types
- correct punctuation of interjections

Editing and Proofreading Marks

∧	Add.
✐	Take out.
⬭ ∧	Move to here.
∧̣	Add comma.
⊙	Add period.

The House of the Future, Here Today

"You won't have to pay another electric bill," the builder said.

"Wait will you say that again?" my sister interrupted.

The builder explained, "Your dishwasher refrigerator oven and stove will all use the power of the sun. Solar cells on the roof change solar energy into electricity."

"Wow what an amazing house!" she exclaimed. "Are there many others like this one?"

"Sure," he replied. "We have built solar houses in Seattle Washington Chicago Illinois and Cleveland Ohio."

Test-Taking Strategy Practice

Read Directions Carefully

Answer the question by choosing the correct answer choice and shading the letter on your answer sheet.

Sample

> **1** Which detail supports this sentence?
>
> Ⓐ Solar cell technology is improving all the time.
>
> ● They used a blanket to insulate the water heater.
>
> Ⓒ Thomas Culhane shows how temperature changes.
>
> Ⓓ The heater has large black panels.

Read the questions about "Energy for the Future." Then write your answers in the space provided.

2 After you eat food, what happens as a result of the chemical reactions inside your body?

_____

3 Where does most of the electrical energy in the world come from?

_____

4 What do the students have to do first in order to build the water heater?

Ⓐ line the box with insulation

Ⓑ test the metal storage tank

Ⓒ build another solar panel

Ⓓ place the tank on a stand

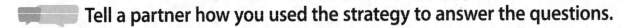 **Tell a partner how you used the strategy to answer the questions.**

Goal-and-Outcome Chart

"Energy for the Future"

Goal	Obstacles	Strategies	Outcome
to use the sun's energy to heat water	BBad weather. Technology could break down.	use in places where it is mostly sunny.	the water will be heated.

→ → →

Use your chart to retell the selection to a partner.

"Energy For the Future"

Use this passage to practice reading with proper phrasing.

Today we had a problem. We tested our metal storage	10
tank. It leaked! Then one student had an idea. He took me to a place	25
where plastic barrels from a shampoo factory were being re-sold. The	36
barrels were inexpensive, and perfect for our hot water heaters.	46
When we returned, the students cheered. "But how will the water	57
in the tank stay hot?" asked one student. "Maybe it just needs a blanket,"	71
said another.	73
Clearly, the students have become energy problem-solvers. At	81
the end of the day today, we insulated our tank with a	93
"blanket" of fiberglass insulation, and then gave each other high-fives.	103

Phrasing

1 ☐ Rarely pauses while reading the text.　　　3 ☐ Frequently pauses at appropriate points in the text.

2 ☐ Occasionally pauses while reading the text.　　4 ☐ Consistently pauses at all appropriate points in the text.

Accuracy and Rate Formula
Use the formula to measure a reader's accuracy and rate while reading aloud.

$$\underline{\hspace{3cm}} - \underline{\hspace{3cm}} = \underline{\hspace{3cm}}$$

words attempted　　　number of errors　　　words correct per minute
in one minute　　　　　　　　　　　　　　　　(wcpm)

Grammar: Reteach

A New England Vacation

Grammar Rules Interjections, Commas in a Series, Semicolons	
Interjections show feelings. • An interjection that shows a strong feeling ends with an **exclamation mark**. • An interjection that shows a mild feeling is followed by a **comma**.	**Hurray!** We're starting our trip today. **Well,** don't forget to visit Boston.
Use **commas** with three or more items in a series. Use a comma before the **coordinating conjunctions** *and* or *or*.	We'll go hiking, swimming, **and** sailing.
When items in a series already contain a comma, use **semicolons** to separate the items.	We'll tour Concord, Massachusetts; Woodstock, Vermont; and Providence, Rhode Island.

Add commas and exclamation marks where they are needed.

1. We got photos maps and souvenirs in New England.

2. Wow Look at this photo of the whale we saw near Nantucket.

3. Well I'd like to visit a European city such as Paris France London England or Rome Italy.

4. Great Let's save our money and go there together some day.

> **Tell a partner about a vacation you want to take. Tell three places to go and what to do in each place.**

Finish My Sentence

To prepare:

1. Collaborate with your partner to write each independent clause and each conjunction below on a separate strip of paper.

2. Place the strips with independent clauses in a cup and place the conjunctions next to the cup.

To play:

1. Player 1 takes a clause from the cup and gives it to Player 2.

2. Player 2 chooses one of the conjunctions. Then, on a blank paper strip, he or she writes a second independent clause that can be added to the first clause using that conjunction. Then, Player 2 combines the three paper strips to form a compound sentence.

3. If Player 1 agrees that the sentence is correct, Player 2 scores 1 point.

4. Players reverse roles and take turns playing until all the clause strips have been used. The player with more points at the end of the game wins.

Independent Clauses

some cities on rivers use water power to create electricity
we get light from the sun
many people use fossil fuels to heat their homes
dark surfaces absorb heat from the sun
solar cells turn light into electricity
wind mills can produce electricity
using solar energy decreases air pollution
fossil fuels cause air pollution

Conjunctions

and	yet	but	or	so

Grammar: Game

Spin a Complex Sentence

Directions:

1. Play with a partner. Take turns.

2. Player 1 spins the spinner and writes a dependent clause using the conjunction that the spinner points to.

3. Player 2 copies down Player 1's dependent clause and adds an independent clause to make a complex sentence.

4. If Player 1 thinks that the sentence is a correct complex sentence, Player 2 scores a point.

5. Then Player 2 takes a turn and spins the spinner. Play continues until partners have completed six sentences. The player with more points at the end wins.

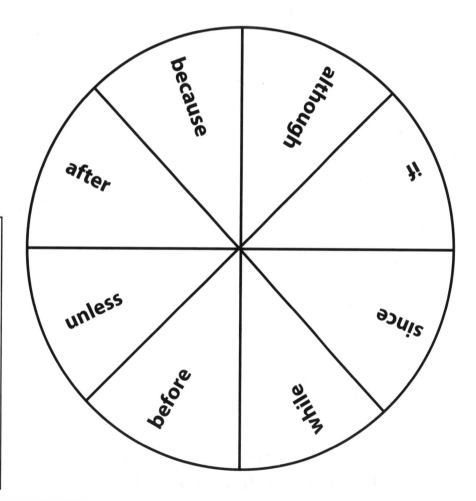

Make a Spinner

1. Put a paper clip over the center of the spinner.
2. Touch the point of a pencil on the middle of the wheel and through the loop of the paper clip.
3. Spin the paper clip to make a spinner.

Comparison Chart

Compare Online Documents

	"How to Make a Solar Oven"	"Energy for the Future"
Genre		
Point of View	first person ☐ second person ☐ third person ☐	first person ☐ second person ☐ third person ☐
Style	slang ☐ exclamation points ☐ abbreviations ☐ questions ☐ conversational voice ☐	slang ☐ exclamation points ☐ abbreviations ☐ questions ☐ conversational voice ☐
Content		

 Talk with a partner about how the purpose of a blog is different from that of a how-to article.

Grammar: Practice

Sun Baked Potatoes

Grammar Rules Compound and Complex Sentences

1. To make a compound sentence, use a comma and a conjunction (*and*, *but*, *or*, *so*, *yet*, or *nor*) to join two independent clauses.

2. Join a dependent clause with an independent clause to make a complex sentence. Use a comma if the dependent clause comes first. Use words such as *when*, *because*, *although*, *while*, and *since*.

Write compound and complex sentences.

_____ you can bake potatoes in an electric or gas oven, it's fun to bake them in the sun! A solar oven may be small _____ it does work. First, wash the potatoes _____ then put them in a pot. The pot must be black _____ it will not absorb enough heat from the sun to cook the potatoes. _____ your potatoes bake, have fun. The pot won't burn _____ your potatoes will take about six hours to bake.

  Write one compound and one complex sentence, and share them with a partner.

Mark-Up Reading

Benefits of Solar Energy

Directions: Write two examples in each circle.

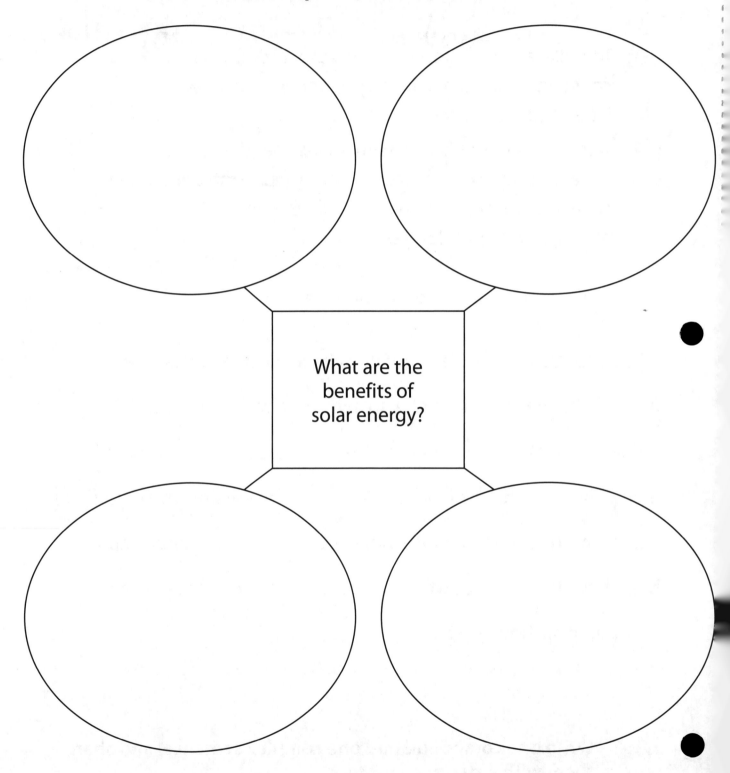

What are the benefits of solar energy?

Name _____ Date _____

Adventures in **SOLAR ENERGY**

| Home | About Me | Archive | Links |

Posted by Nick Tsuruda

May 4, 2011

Welcome to my blog! My name is Nick, and I have decided to install solar panels on my house. The panels will absorb sunlight that can power my house. It costs to install the panels, but after that, the electricity they provide is free! I have to wonder though, will my power go out at night or on rainy days?

▲ Solar panels covering the roof of the house convert sunlight into electricity

May 5, 2011

Today, I met with Cynthia, who installs solar panels. She explained that the system stores the sun's energy in batteries that generate electricity, but my house will still be connected to the city power grid. On cloudy days, my panels might not generate enough power, so the power company's system takes over. What if the solar panels produce more electricity than I need? The excess current is transmitted back into the grid and can be used by my neighbors! How incredible is that?

Cynthia will install solar panels on the south side of my house, where the sun's rays are the strongest. She made sure that there are no trees or buildings that could send shadows over the panels. Luckily, my roof has a clear opening to the sky!

Mark-Up Reading

Adventures in SOLAR ENERGY

| Home | About Me | Archive | Links |

May 25, 2011

The installation is complete! My solar energy system is up and running. Today is a beautiful sunny day, and I can almost feel the electricity being created for free. Yesterday, I saw my electric meter running backwards! That means I'm selling electricity to the power company. I can't wait to get my electricity bill next month—I know it will decrease significantly. The PV cells cost a lot, but they will pay for themselves down the road with the money I save on electricity.

▲ I generated so much electricity that it went back through the grid to the city. And my meter ran backwards!

May 27, 2011

I've been thinking about more benefits of my solar energy system. The power company has to burn coal in order to make electricity. But burning coal also produces gases that pollute the air. One benefit of solar energy is that it does not produce air pollution. So if more people used solar energy, the air we all breathe would be cleaner!

One of my neighbors stopped by. Now, he sees the wisdom of buying a solar energy system to heat the water for his pool. Water heating is one of the most common uses of solar energy here in the United States.

Keep checking in to my blog to see how many watts I produce each month with my own personal power company! Thanks for visiting!

Solar Cookers
by Kate Levine

NYAKACH, KENYA – When your family cooks a meal, they probably use a stove or microwave, right? These appliances run on gas or electricity. In rural Africa, many people use wood fires to cook. Wood can be expensive or hard to find. Some women walk miles to gather enough to cook dinner!

▲ A woman uses a solar oven to cook dinner.

Now, people without electricity have an alternative to wood: the sun! Solar Cookers International (SCI) is helping people in Kenya reduce their use of limited resources such as wood and reduce pollution from wood smoke.

SCI makes a type of solar cooker called a panel oven. It can be made out of inexpensive materials, such as cardboard and aluminum foil. A panel oven can cost as little as $7! Since it uses only the sun to make thermal energy, it runs for free after that.

Solar cookers are safer than cooking fires. And in places where clean drinking water is hard to find, some solar cookers produce enough heat to purify water.

One disadvantage to solar cookers is increased cooking time. Panel cookers can take three hours to cook a meal. You also can't cook at night. But even with intermittent use, there are huge benefits to using solar cookers.

Grammar: Grammar and Writing

Edit and Proofread

Choose the Editing and Proofreading Marks you need to correct the passage. Look for the following:

- correct compound sentences
- correct complex sentences
- correct use of commas and conjunctions

Editing and Proofreading Marks

∧	Add.
℘	Take out.
⌒ ∧	Move to here.
⋏	Add comma.
⊙	Add period.

How to Build a Solar Panel

Heating water requires energy, *and* that energy can come from the sun. To make a solar panel, start by building a box. The box can be made out of any material it should be easy to carry up to your roof.

First, build metal pipes into the box to hold the water. The solar panel will have to store heat the box should be insulated.

The solar panel should be coated with light-absorbing paint. Light colors reflect sunlight but dark colors absorb it. Black is probably the best choice. When you have your solar panel you can rely on the sun for hot water!

Pets

Grammar Rules **Compound and Complex Sentences**	
A compound sentence is made up of two or more **independent clauses**. They are connected with a comma and a **coordinating conjunction**: *and, but, or, so, for, yet*, and *nor*.	Ian has an aquarium, **and** he fills it with saltwater fish.
A complex sentence has an independent clause and one or more dependent clauses. A **dependent clause** begins with a **subordinating conjunction**: *after, before, because, if, since, when, where,* and *while*.	Many people like fish as pets **because** fish are easy to take care of. **If** I wanted a pet, I would get a dog **because** dogs are so loving and fun.

**Read each sentence. Underline the dependent clauses.
Then write if the sentence is compound or complex.**

1. Before I chose a dog, I researched different breeds. _____

2. Poodles are very smart, but they can be expensive. _____

3. If I go to the shelter, I will find a dog. _____

4. Mom and I went to PetZ, and we found a great dog! _____

5. Because the dog was so happy, we named him Sparky. _____

Talk about pets with your partner. Use compound and complex sentences.

Unit Concept Map

Nature's Network

**Make a concept map with the answers to the Big Question:
What is nature's network?**

What is nature's network?

Name _____ Date _____

Retell a Story

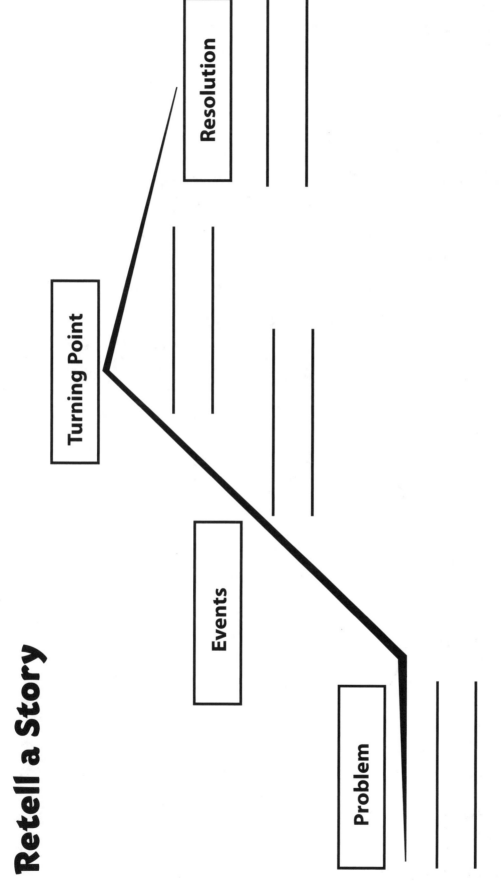

Resolution

Turning Point

Events

Problem

Retell an animal story you know or have experienced. Use this plot diagram to help you plan your story.

For use with TE p. T153a

PM3.2

Unit 3 | Nature's Network

Grammar: Game

Spin and Name It

Directions:

1. **Play with a partner.**

2. **Take turns spinning the paper clip.**

3. **When the spinner stops on one of the categories, name a proper noun that fits that category of noun.**

4. **If your partner agrees that your proper noun is correct, write it on a piece of paper.**

5. **Play until one player has ten correct proper nouns.**

6. **Share your lists with another pair of students.**

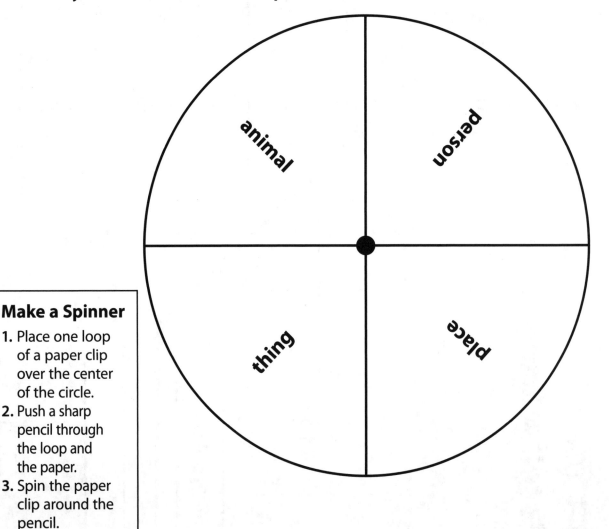

Make a Spinner

1. Place one loop of a paper clip over the center of the circle.
2. Push a sharp pencil through the loop and the paper.
3. Spin the paper clip around the pencil.

Grammar: Grammar and Writing

Edit and Proofread

Choose the Editing and Proofreading Marks you need to correct the passage. Look for the following:

- correct use of common and proper nouns
- correct capitalization of common and proper nouns
- correct use of the articles *a, an, the*

Editing and Proofreading Marks

∧	Add.
ℓ	Take out.
≡	Capitalize.
/	Make lowercase.
⊙	Add period.

Our Family visited New Mexico last year. I especially liked a Place

called tent Rocks National Monument. It is in the desert and is dry

and sandy.

We hiked through a narrow Arroyo and climbed an bluff. Along

the way, my sister, megan, saw a chipmunk. Then we spotted an

lizard. The lizard stared at us before it raced away.

Then I saw a animal that I'll always remember. It was a Coyote!

ranger Claire said there are many of them in Tent Rocks. I will always

remember our trip to new mexico because of that coyote.

Test-Taking Strategy Practice

Look for Important Words

Directions: Read each question about "Coyote and Badger." Choose the best answer.

Sample

1 What happens before Coyote and Badger start hunting together?

   Ⓐ   Everyone eats a big meal.

   Ⓑ   An eagle takes Badger's pup.

   ●   There is no rain.

   Ⓓ   Coyote howls with other coyotes.

2 Why do Coyote and Badger hunt together?

   Ⓐ   They catch more animals.

   Ⓑ   Every hunt is successful.

   Ⓒ   They were lonely before.

   Ⓓ   They couldn't catch anything before they hunted together.

3 Why is the rain important to Coyote and Badger?

   Ⓐ   There is not enough rain.

   Ⓑ   Coyote and Badger decide to hunt together.

   Ⓒ   Coyote sleeps during the day.

   Ⓓ   Plants will grow, and there will be more prey.

 Tell a partner how you used the strategy to answer the questions.

Plot Diagram

"Coyote and Badger"

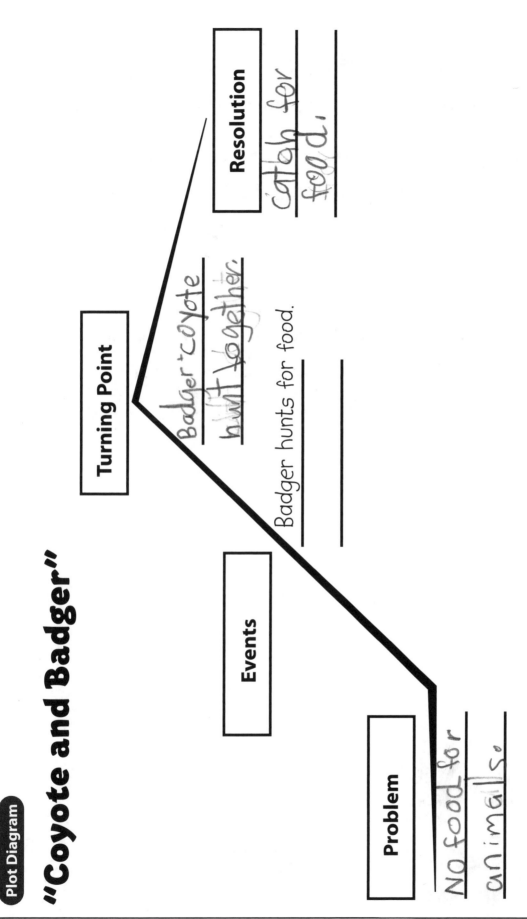

Turning Point

Resolution

catch for food.

Badger+coyote hunt together.

Badger hunts for food.

Events

Problem

No food for animals.

Use your plot diagram to retell the story to a partner.

Fluency Practice

"Coyote and Badger"

Use this passage to practice reading with proper intonation.

Farther up the canyon, Badger emerged from her den. She left her two | 13

pups safely underground and waddled off as the air began to cool. | 25

Badger was a night hunter, too, but she seldom chased rabbits. | 36

She was a digger, not a runner. | 43

When Badger found the hole of an antelope squirrel, she tore into the | 56

hard soil with her long claws. The dirt flew, and in a wink she was | 71

underground following a dark tunnel. No animal can dig as fast as | 83

a badger, but the squirrel raced ahead and escaped. | 92

Intonation

| 1 | ☐ Does not change pitch.
| 2 | ☐ Changes pitch, but does not match content.
| 3 | ☐ Changes pitch to match some of the content.
| 4 | ☐ Changes pitch to match all of the content.

Accuracy and Rate Formula
Use the formula to measure a reader's accuracy and rate while reading aloud.

| _____ | − | _____ | = | _____ |
| words attempted in one minute | | number of errors | | words correct per minute (wcpm) |

Grammar: Reteach

Searching for Acorns

Grammar Rules Common and Proper Nouns

A **common noun** names a general person, animal, place, thing, or idea. Capitalize common nouns that begin a sentence.	Dogs like chasing squirrels.
A **proper noun** names a particular person, animal, place, thing, or idea. Capitalize all important words in a proper noun.	My dog Max chases squirrels in Patterson Park on Third Street.

Read the sentences. Circle the common nouns. Underline letters that should be capitalized.

1. There is a shortage of acorns in the town of fairhaven, new York.

2. The town's librarian, mitchell rosen, says that many towns east of the mississippi river are having the same problem.

3. animals that cannot store enough food, cannot survive.

4. A scientist at greenhill college says that an oak tree does not produce the same amount of acorns each year.

5. In a year when acorns are few, the food chain that depends on them suffers.

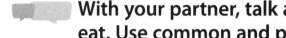 **With your partner, talk about what different kinds of animals eat. Use common and proper nouns.**

Grammar: Game

Make Them Plural

Directions:

1. Play with a partner.

2. Use a paper clip, eraser, or other small object as a game marker and place it on START.

3. Flip a coin to move. Heads = 1 space; Tails = 2 spaces.

4. Read the noun on the space where you land, and write its plural form.

5. If your partner agrees that you spelled the plural form correctly, stay where you are. If not, go back one space. If you disagree, check the spelling in a dictionary.

6. Take turns. The first player to reach the END is the winner.

START	carnivore	branch	berry	coyote
				bush
breeze	butterfly	monkey	bee	jelly
consumer				
mosquito	turkey	burrow	ax	END

Grammar: Game

Nouns That End in *f* or *fe*

Directions:

1. Play in teams of two or three. Two teams will play against each other.

2. First, work with your opposing team to write each noun in the boxes below on a separate index card. Then shuffle the cards and stack them face down.

3. Teams take turns with the other team drawing a card from the top of the stack.

4. Read the noun on the card, and spell its plural form. Check the spelling in a dictionary. If the spelling is correct, your team gets one point.

5. Place the card at the bottom of the stack and continue playing.

6. Play until one team has won ten points.

life	half	leaf	safe	self
wharf	shelf	giraffe	thief	wife
belief	proof	wolf	calf	gulf

Compare Content

Add the names of plants and animals from "Coyote and Badger" to correct places in the food web.

Food Web

badger

coyote

Talk to a partner about how the animals and plants in this food web are connected.

Grammar: Practice

What Do They Eat?

Grammar Rules Plural Nouns

1. Add -s to make most nouns pural.

   plant → plant<u>s</u>

2. Add -es to nouns that end in *x, ch, sh, ss, z,* and sometimes *o.*

   branch → branch<u>es</u>

3. For **most** nouns that end in *y,* change the *y* to *i* and then add -es.

   berry → berr<u>ies</u>

4. For **most** nouns that end in *f* or *fe,* change the *f* or *fe* to *v* and then add -es.

   life → liv<u>es</u>

Write the plural nouns.

1. A potato plant is a producer. It produces roots, stems, and ___leaves___ .
   (leaf)

2. Some animals eat potato _____ .
   (plant)

3. They need the energy in the _____ to survive.
   (potato)

4. Animals such as _____ also eat other animals.
   (fox)

5. Eagles sometimes eat badger _____ .
   (baby)

Name _____ Date _____

Mark-Up Reading

Types of Rain Forests by Sharon Sanchez

There are two types of rain forests, tropical and temperate. Both grow in wet climates and have similar damp soils. Tropical rain forests are found in hot regions near the Equator. Temperate rain forests develop in higher latitudes with cooler temperatures.

A tropical rain forest is covered by a tight canopy formed by the interlocking branches of huge trees with large leaves. In contrast, a temperate rain forest has a lower, less dense growth of trees.

▲ tropical rain forest

▲ temperate rain forest

The Forest Floor by Edward Calvert

The dense canopy of a tropical rain forest affects the life beneath it. The canopy is like an umbrella that hides and protects the layers below. As a result, very little light reaches the forest floor, so plants on the forest floor compete with one another for light and space. Few plants and shrubs can grow in this dim light. Vines are common because they are able to climb up tree trunks to reach the light. In the darkest parts of the forest, brilliantly colored fungi thrive in conditions that are unfavorable to most other plants.

"Types of Rain Forests"	Both	"The Forest Floor"
Signal Words		**Signal Words**

Mark-Up Reading

What's on the Menu? by Valerie Kasiske

In the tropical rain forest, how high up you are might determine what's for dinner! In the canopy, monkeys and parrots feed mainly on fruit, leaves, and seeds. Some of this same food falls to the ground. But on the hot, damp forest floor, the fruit, leaves, and seeds quickly rot. This means that the forest floor has much more food for decomposers.

Although the forest floor swarms with tiny decomposers, it is also home to the largest rainforest predators, including the jaguar. While the canopy has far fewer large predators, these predators still make an impact on the food chain. For example, harpy eagles from the canopy prey on tree-dwellers such as sloths and monkeys.

While the menus of the canopy and forest floor are different, some animals, like the long-tailed raccoon-like coati, move freely between the zones in order to take advantage of both menus. Residents of the tropical rainforest can transform their menus simply by moving up or down in their world!

◀ Different plants and animals live in the rainforest canopy than on the forest floor.

Name _____ Date _____

Small Food Web—Big Trouble! by Erin Ming

Brrrrr! Snow covers the cold Arctic. As a result, only a limited number of species can survive there. That means the Arctic food web is very small. A small food web tends to be unstable. If the Arctic food web falls out of balance, the whole living network of the Arctic environment could begin to unravel. What factors keep this fragile food web stable?

▲ Reindeer eat small plants and bushes.

Arctic Producers

Producers play an important role in the Arctic food web. Since they are at the bottom of the web, they provide energy to all other species. So, the number of consumers depends on the number of producers. Temperatures drop as you travel north from Alaska toward the North Pole. Because of this, the number of leafy plant species also drops dramatically. Small low-growing plants like shrubs, lichens, and mosses are more common than leafy plants.

Arctic Consumers

As you move northward, the effect of colder temperatures and fewer producers is a decrease in animal species. There are only about 45 species of mammals in the Arctic. Some, like caribou (reindeer), eat a lot of plants. A change in plant life can greatly affect their numbers. A change in the number of caribou can then affect the number of wolves, one of their main predators. Such changes can deform the small, fragile Arctic food web.

Small Food Web—Big Trouble! (continued)

A Keystone Species

Small food webs tend to be unstable because species depend so much on one another to survive. Sometimes food webs rely on a specific animal so much that it is called a keystone species. In the Arctic, one keystone species is a small herbivore: the lemming.

Every three or four years, large numbers of lemmings are born. Because there is more prey, the number of lemming predators, such as Arctic foxes and snowy owls, also rises. These small carnivores in turn provide food for bigger carnivores, such as wolves, causing their populations to grow. However, when the lemmings' numbers are small, there isn't enough food to go around. As a result, smaller predators and their larger predators are both in danger of starving.

"What's on the Menu?"	Both	"Small Food Web—Big Trouble!"
Signal Words		**Signal Words**

Grammar: Grammar and Writing

Edit and Proofread

Choose the Editing and Proofreading Marks you need to correct the passage. Look for the following:

- correct use of plural nouns
- correct spelling of plural nouns
- correct punctuation

Editing and Proofreading Marks

∧	Add.
℘	Take out.
⊂⊃ ∧	Move to here.
∧̣	Add comma.
⊙	Add period.

Several month ^s^ ago my uncle took me to a lake with some marshs to see the birds. We wore high boot to protect our feet and calfs. Wading through muddy water we pushed through tall grasss and bushs. Gnats flyes and mosquitos swarmed around us.

When we got to a tiny island we took out our binoculares and looked around. It was amazing! Hundreds of duck swam on the lake. Two hawkes circled overhead. Across the lake eagles soared above the line of cliff. Bitten by all those insect, I itched for six day, but I have great memoryes from that trip!

Grammar: Reteach

Chef Ramon

Grammar Rules Plural Nouns

To make a noun plural: Add **-s** to most nouns.	table napkin	→ →	tab**les** napkin**s**
Add **-es** to nouns that end in **x**, **ch**, **sh**, **ss**, **z**, and sometimes **o**.	box tomato	→ →	box**es** tomat**oes**
For most nouns that end in **y**, change to **y** to **i** and add **-es**.	penny babies	→ →	penn**ies** bab**ies**
For words that end with a vowel then **y**, just add **-s**.	way bay	→ →	way**s** bay**s**
For many nouns that end with **f** or **fe**, drop the **f** or **fe** and add **–ves**.	knife half	→ →	kni**ves** hal**ves**
For some nouns that end with **f** or **fe**, just add an **–s**.	café roof	→ →	café**s** roof**s**

Circle the word that correctly completes each sentence.

1. Ramon cooks hundreds of (dishes/dishs) every day.
2. His (dayes/days) at the cafe are very busy.
3. Everyone loves Ramon's cooking and the (spicees/spices) he uses.
4. Cooks from other (citys/cities) come in to see Ramon.
5. They like to share the best recipes from other (cafés/caves).

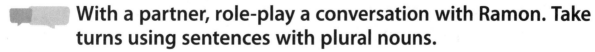 **With a partner, role-play a conversation with Ramon. Take turns using sentences with plural nouns.**

Tree Diagram

Small Things, Big Idea!

Use the tree diagram below to track the details your partner gives about why a small plant or animal is important.

Main Idea	**Details**

 Have your partner review your tree diagram and make suggestions for possible additions.

Grammar: Game

Spin for the Title

Directions:

1. Play with a partner. Take turns.

2. Spin the paper clip. Punctuate and capitalize the title that you land on.

3. Win two points for correct punctuation and capitalization. Subtract one point for incorrect punctuation or capitalization. Spin again if you land on a title that has already been written correctly.

4. After all titles have been used, the partner with more points wins.

> **Make a Spinner**
> 1. Place one loop of a paper clip over the center of the circle.
> 2. Push a sharp pencil through the loop and the paper.
> 3. Spin the paper clip around the pencil.

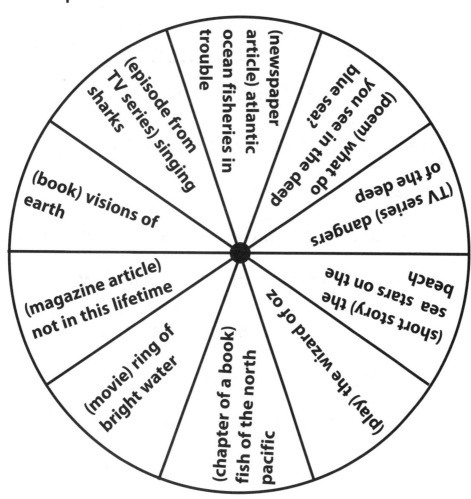

Grammar: Grammar and Writing

Edit and Proofread

Choose the Editing and Proofreading Marks you need to correct the passage. Look for the following:

- correct punctuation and capitalization of titles
- correct agreement of verbs with colllective nouns

Editing and Proofreading Marks

∧	Add.
ℒ	Take out.
≡	Capitalize.
/	Make lowercase.
——	Italicize or underline.

I am fascinated by sharks. When our family go∧ to the city
(es added above go)

aquarium, I head straight to the shark exhibit.

I started liking sharks when I saw the movie "Jaws." Now I take

a class about sharks at the aquarium, and I learn from realistic TV

shows like Shark men. My favorite episode is Blood In The Water. It is

about a team that try to capture and study a great white shark.

Our class are reading a book called "Great white sharks." I like

a chapter called Status about why sharks are endangered. If more

people read that chapter, they might try to protect sharks.

Name _____   Date _____

Look for Important Words

Directions: Read each question about "Fish of the Future." Choose the best answer.

Sample

> **1** What happens after the tag releases from the sunfish's body?
>
> Ⓐ It sinks to the bottom.
>
> ● It floats to the surface.
>
> Ⓒ It attaches to another fish.
>
> Ⓓ It follows the sunfish.

2 How does the sunfish eat jellyfish?

Ⓐ The sunfish uses its caudal fins to eat the jellyfish.

Ⓑ The sunfish dives deep into the water many times a day.

Ⓒ The sunfish sucks the jellyfish in and out of its mouth until it breaks.

Ⓓ The jellyfish swim directly into the sunfish's mouth.

3 What has a negative affect on the food web?

Ⓐ technology

Ⓑ plankton

Ⓒ sunfish

Ⓓ overfishing

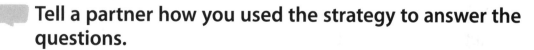 **Tell a partner how you used the strategy to answer the questions.**

Tree Diagram

"Fish of the Future"

	It has a strange body shape.
p. 194–196 What's special about the sunfish?	It lies on its side at the ocean's surface as if it's sunning itself.
What's pg 195 Special about the sunfish?	It has a beak-like mouth.
	It is covered with parasites.
The sunfish and their ocean food web predators except humans. Pg. 198.	The sunfish eats jellyfish.
	Adult sunfish's huge size protects it from predators. Except humans.
An ocean food web Pg. 201	The sunfish has the potential to keep jellyfish population under control.

 With a partner, use your tree diagrams to determine the main idea of the interview.

Fluency Practice

"Fish of the Future"

Use this passage to practice reading with proper expression.

The sunfish holds three world records! As it grows, the sunfish	11
increases in weight more than any other vertebrate—up to 60 million	23
times its size at hatching. If you grew that much, you'd be as big as 30	39
thousand school buses!	42
Second, it is the world's heaviest bony fish. The heaviest sunfish ever	54
recorded weighed more than 2,300 kilograms (over 5,000 pounds).	63
That's as heavy as ten grand pianos, or five large cows!	74
Third, the sunfish produces more eggs at one time than any other	86
vertebrate. Scientists found one mother sunfish carrying an estimated	95
300 million eggs.	98

Intonation

1 ☐ Does not read with feeling.	3 ☐ Reads with appropriate feeling for most content.
2 ☐ Reads with some feeling, but does not match content.	4 ☐ Reads with appropriate feeling for all content.

Accuracy and Rate Formula
Use the formula to measure a reader's accuracy and rate while reading aloud.

_____ − _____ = _____
words attempted   number of errors   words correct per minute
in one minute   (wcpm)

Name _____ Date _____

Fantasy Animals

Grammar Rules Titles, Collective Nouns

Italicize titles of books, plays, movies, and TV series if you type. If you are handwriting, <u>underline</u> them. Capitalize all words in a title, except for articles, short conjunctions, and prepositions.	*Charlotte's Web* <u>Charlotte's Web</u> <u>T</u>he <u>Cat</u> in the <u>Hat</u> <u>Into</u> the <u>Unknown</u>
Use a **collective noun** to name a group of people, animals, or things. • If a **collective noun** refers to a group acting as one, use a **singular verb**. • If a **collective noun** shows members of a group acting separately, use a **plural verb**.	In <u>Charlotte's Web</u>, an animal **community** <u>lives</u> in a barn. The **majority** of animals <u>talk</u> to Wilbur, the pig.

Proofread the sentences. Correct any errors in punctuation, capitalization, and subject/verb agreement.

1. The fantasy novel watership down tells what happens when a rabbit community are threatened.

2. The group disagree about how to protect themselves.

3. The TV series redwall was based on novels by brian jacques.

4. In the novel the rogue crew, an animal team defend an abbey.

 With your partner, talk about your favorite books.

Noun Spin

Directions:

1. Play with two or three classmates. Take turns.

2. Spin the spinner. Identify the word the spinner points to as a count, noncount, or collective noun, and then cross off that word on the spinner.

3. Write a sentence using the noun. Say whether you have used the noun to talk about one thing or more than one thing.

4. If the other players think you have identified the noun correctly, score one point. If they agree that your sentence is correct, score an additional point.

5. Play until all the words have been used. The player with the most points at the end wins.

Make a Spinner

1. Place one loop of a paper clip over the center of the circle.
2. Push a sharp pencil through the loop and the paper.
3. Spin the paper clip around the pencil.

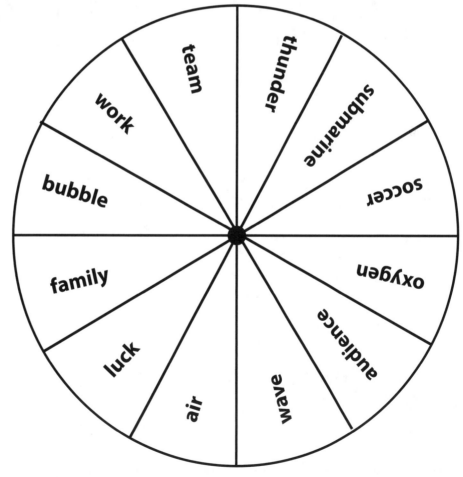

Grammar: Game

It's Irregular

Directions:

1. Play with a partner.

2. Use a paper clip, eraser, or other small object as a game piece.

3. Flip a coin to move. Heads = 1 space; Tails = 2 spaces.

4. Read the irregular noun on the space where you land. Write its plural form.

5. Check your spelling in a dictionary. If you spelled the plural form correctly, stay where you are. If you did not spell it correctly, go back one space.

6. Take turns. The first to reach FINISH is the winner.

START	mouse	sheep
		child
tooth	man	ox
moose		
species	FINISH	

Compare Genres

Use this chart to compare "Phyto-Power!" with "Fish of the Future."

	Science Article	**Interview**
Purpose Is the purpose to inform, entertain, or persuade?		
Text Structure	Main Idea and Details	Question and Answer
	Photos **Tables** **Charts** **Illustrations** **Headings** **Maps** **Diagrams**	**Photos** **Tables** **Charts** **Illustrations** **Headings** **Maps** **Diagrams**

 Take turns with a partner. Ask each other questions about an interview or a science article.

Grammar: Practice

The Make-It-Plural Game

Grammar Rules **Plural Nouns**

1. Some nouns are the same for "one" and "more than one."

   a grain of sand ➜ all the grains of sand

2. Some nouns have special spellings for "more than one."

   one mouse ➜ two mice

3. Collective nouns name groups of people or things.
   To make these nouns plural, add -s or -es.

   one collection of seashells ➜ two collections of seashells

Directions:

1. **Play with a partner.**

2. **Spin the spinner.**

3. **Change the noun to a plural noun. If the plural form is the same as the singular, say:** *same form.* **Say a sentence using the plural noun.**

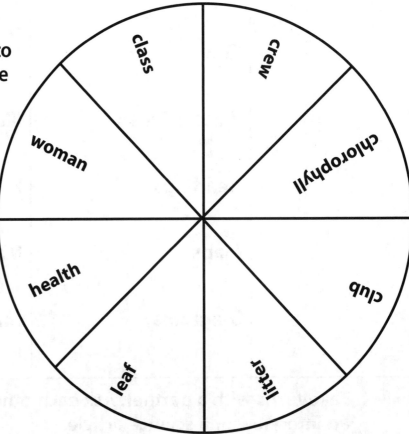

Make a Spinner

1. Put a paper clip through the center of the circle.
2. Hold one end of the paper clip with a pencil.
3. Spin the paper clip around the pencil.

For use with TE p. T214a

Unit 3 | Nature's Network

Mark-Up Reading

Shark Tidbits! by Paul Hennessey

Imagine you are swimming, and hear something behind you. To see it, you would have to turn around, right? Not if you were a hammerhead shark! 360-degree vision is just one of the unusual features found in some sharks, and there are many more. For example, did you know that the biggest shark eats mainly tiny plankton? Or that a great white shark can replace its teeth?

Stated or Implied ?

Main Idea _____

_____

One unusual feature of great white sharks is their ability to protect their eyes when attacking prey. Keen eyesight is important to these sharks, so they must prevent damage to their eyes. To keep their eyes from being injured, great whites can roll their eyes back into their heads.

Stated or Implied?

Main Idea _____

_____

Now let's look inside a great white shark's mouth. This fierce predator has more than 3,000 razor-sharp teeth arranged in rows. It uses its teeth to rip out chunks of flesh from its prey. But instead of chewing its food, it swallows the bites whole! So why so many teeth? The inner rows of teeth are just for back-up. If a tooth in the front row breaks or falls out, a tooth from the next row moves forward to take its place!

▲ Great white sharks have rows of sharp teeth.

Stated or Implied ?

Main Idea _____

_____

Shark Tidbits! (continued)

Speaking of meals, you might think that the enormous whale shark would prey on enormous fish, but just the opposite is true. The biggest fish in the ocean feeds only on tiny food. This gentle giant moves slowly through the water sucking water through its gills like an ocean vacuum cleaner. The gills filter out tiny marine life that the shark then swallows and eats. These gulps of food include plankton, small fish, fish eggs, and larvae.

▲ The largest shark eats the tiniest organisms in the ocean.

Stated or Implied?

Main Idea _____

_____

Even though sharks have so many fascinating features, some people just see sharks as something to fear. People often picture sharks terrorizing helpless swimmers. However, sharks kill fewer than 25 humans a year. Compare that to the 73 million sharks killed each year by humans. So who is the greater predator?

Stated or Implied ?

Main Idea _____

_____

Grammar: Grammar and Writing

Edit and Proofread

Choose the Editing and Proofreading Marks you need to correct the passage. Look for the following:

- correct use of irregular plural nouns
- correct use of collective nouns
- correct use of count and noncount nouns

Editing and Proofreading Marks

∧	Add.
ꟼ	Take out.
≡	Capitalize.
/	Make lowercase.

My class study the ocean. Last week we went to an aquarium. *(ies added above "study")*

The waters in the aquarium was really clear. I could see all of the

fishes. I especially liked watching a school of parrotfish. The school

were fun to watch.

We also took a boat ride out to sea. The sunshines were bright!

We saw a pod of six whales. A pod are a group of whales. One

teacher exclaimed, "The pod is rolling in the water and swimming

closer to our boat!" There were many school childs on the boat, but I

think the teachers enjoyed the adventure just as much.

Next month the class are going to the zoo. I will see many kinds

of animals, such as deers, bisons, goose, and even mooses.

Grammar: Reteach

Fundraising Fun

Grammar Rules Irregular Plurals

Collective nouns name a group. • When the group acts together, use a <u>singular</u> <u>verb</u>. • When the group members act as individuals, use a <u>plural</u> <u>verb</u>.	The soccer **team** plans a bake sale. The **team** bring in their baked goods.
Noncount nouns do not have plural forms. Always use a <u>singular verb</u> with noncount nouns.	**Rain** is expected, so the sale will be indoors
Irregular nouns do not follow the usual rules for forming plurals • Some have a special spelling for plurals. • Others have the same spelling for both singular and plural.	Many **men** and **women** buy my cookies. Some of the cookies are shaped like **sheep**.

Proofread the sentences. Correct any errors in spelling and subject/verb agreement.

1. A lot of moneys are raised by groups in our community.

2. Our class want to raise money to help childs in disaster areas.

3. The class brings in contributions from our friends and family.

4. Some mans in our town are raising money for a playground.

With your partner, talk about a fundraising event. Use as many kinds of plural nouns as you can.

Justice

Make a concept map with the answers to the Big Question: What is justice?

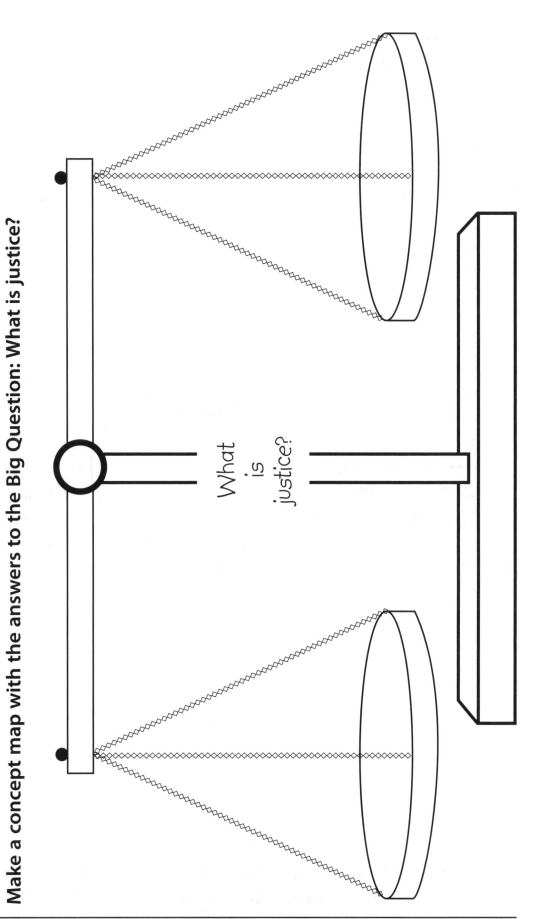

What is justice?

Name _____ Date _____

TV Show: _____

Theme Chart

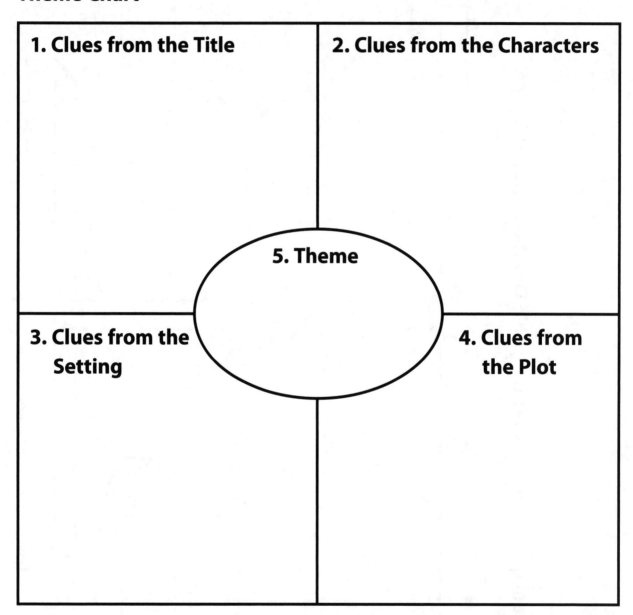

1. Clues from the Title	2. Clues from the Characters
3. Clues from the Setting	4. Clues from the Plot

5. Theme

 Talk with a partner about a television show you have seen about a hero. Together, decide what you think the theme is.

Fluency Practice

"Crossing Bok Chitto"

Use this passage to practice reading with proper expression.

Then one day trouble came. Twenty enslaved people	8
were going to be sold. The men were called together to	19
listen to the names being read. Little Mo's mother was on	30
that list.	32
Little Mo's father wondered how to tell his family.	41
After supper, he motioned for them to be still. Feeling	51
his knees grow weak, he said, "Your mother has been	61
sold."	62
"Nooo!" she cried. The children began to cry, too.	71
"This is our last evening together!" he said. "Stop your	81
crying. I want every one of you to find something small	92
and precious to give your mother to remember you by."	102
No one moved.	105

Intonation

1 ☐ Does not read with feeling.

2 ☐ Reads with some feeling, but does not match content.

3 ☐ Reads with appropriate feeling for most content.

4 ☐ Reads with appropriate feeling for all content.

Accuracy and Rate Formula
Use the formula to measure a reader's accuracy and rate while reading aloud.

_____ − _____ = _____
words attempted   number of errors   words correct per minute
in one minute   (wcpm)

Grammar: Reteach

The Race

Grammar Rules Transitive/Intransitive Verbs

A **transitive verb** needs an **object** to complete its meaning. • The **object** is a noun or pronoun that receives the action of the verb. • The **object** of a transitive verb answers *whom?* or *what?*	Coach **schedules** a team practice. The team **meets him** at the school.
An **intransitive verb** does not need an object. • It can end a sentence. • It may be followed by other words that tell <u>how</u>, <u>where</u>, or <u>when</u>.	We **stretch**. We **walk** <u>slowly</u> up to the starting line.

Read each sentence. Circle the verb. Tell if it is *transitive* or *intransitive*.

1. Coach finds the whistle. _____

2. He sets the stopwatch. _____

3. The whistle blows. _____

4. We race as fast as we can. _____

5. Coach smiles proudly. _____

6. Our race times beat the school record! _____

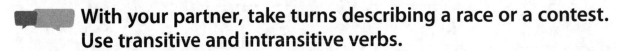 **With your partner, take turns describing a race or a contest. Use transitive and intransitive verbs.**

Grammar: Game

Spin a Link

Directions:

1. Play with a partner. Take turns.

2. Spin the spinner. Complete the sentence frame the spinner points to. What is this sentence missing? Either add the missing linking verb or the missing word or words that should follow the verb. Choose your linking verbs from the box.

3. If your partner thinks you have completed the sentence correctly, score one point.

4. Play until all the sentence frames have been used. The player with the most points at the end wins.

be	feel
am	feels
was	felt
were	smell
look	smells
looks	smelled
looked	taste
seem	tastes
seems	tasted
seemed	

Make a Spinner

1. Put a paper clip over the center of the spinner.
2. Touch the point of a pencil on the middle of the wheel and through the loop of the paper clip.
3. Spin the paper clip to make a spinner.

Grammar: Game

Linking Verb Bingo

To prepare:

1. Choose one student in your group to be the "Caller." The other students are "Players."

2. Players write each of the nine listed verbs in random order in a separate box on the bingo card below.

3. The Caller writes a sentence for each verb, using the verb as a linking verb or as a verb that is not linking. Not all sentences should have linking verbs. Then the Caller mixes up the sentences.

To play:

1. The Caller reads a sentence.

2. Players put a marker on a square that contains the verb plus the correct way that the verb was used in the sentence. (Example: For the sentence *I smell smoke, smell* would be a "not linking" verb)

3. The first Player to get three in a row (vertically, horizontally, or diagonally) calls "Bingo!" If the words covered on the Bingo card match the words used in the Caller's sentences, that player wins.

look remain feel grow smell become appear seem taste	_____ Linking	_____ Not Linking	_____ Linking
	_____ Not Linking	_____ Linking	_____ Not Linking
	_____ Linking	_____ Not Linking	_____ Linking

Voices of the Underground Railroad

Levi Coffin

Account of Levi Coffin, a white male conductor on the Underground Railroad:

In the winter of 1826–27, fugitives began coming to our house. They would find a welcome and be forwarded safely on their journey. Friends in the neighborhood, who used to be fearful of the penalty of the law, were [felt] encouraged to help the escaping slaves when they saw the fearless manner in which I acted.

My neighbors would clothe the fugitives and would aid in forwarding them on their way, but were timid about sheltering them under their roof. So, we did that part of the work. Some in the neighborhood seemed really glad to see the work go on, if somebody else would do it. Others tried to discourage me from running such risks.

Account of Sam Davis, an African-American male slave who escaped to Canada:

I travelled on three days and nights, suffering for want of food. When I was passing through Orangetown, Pennsylvania, two men followed me with muskets. By and by, watching my chance, I jumped a fence and ran. I ran into the woods and then into a wheat field, where I lay all day—from 9 a.m. until dark. I could not sleep for fear.

Mark-Up Reading

Voices of the Underground Railroad (continued)

Account of Charles Peyton Lucas, an African-American male slave who escaped to the North:

We came to a white man who was asleep. We knew nothing of the way, so we decided to awaken him. He said we were runaways, so I expected trouble. The man approached us. Had he tried to touch us we would have defended ourselves, but he proved to be the best friend we ever had. We followed his directions and soon found the Underground Railroad.

Account of Harriet Tubman, an African-American female slave who escaped and then helped hundreds of other slaves escape:

When I found I had crossed that line into free territory, I looked at my hands to see if I was the same person. There was such a glory! The sun came like gold through the trees, and over the fields, and I felt like I was in Heaven. I was free; but there was no one to welcome me to the land of freedom. I was a stranger in a strange land. My home, after all, was down in Maryland because my father, mother, brothers and sisters, and friends were there. But I was free, and they should be free.

▲ Harriet Tubman, who escaped from slavery herself, helped hundreds of slaves escape to freedom on the Underground Railroad.

Mark-Up Reading

Voices of the
Underground Railroad (continued)

Narrator's Viewpoint

Narrator	Details	What This Shows About the Narrator's Viewpoint
Levi Coffin	• welcomed fugitives • forwarded them to safety • was fearless	• felt slaves should be free
Neighbors	• fearful of the law • felt encouraged to help	
Sam Davis	• suffered to escape • could not sleep for fear • afraid of being caught	• felt slaves should be free
Charles Peyton Lucas	• expected trouble • ready to defend himself • helped by a stranger	
Harriet Tubman	• freedom felt like Heaven • freedom also felt strange • felt all should be free • helped slaves escape	

Grammar: Grammar and Writing

Edit and Proofread

Choose the Editing and Proofreading Marks you need to correct the passage. Look for the following:

- missing linking verbs
- correct use of linking verbs
- correct subject-verb agreement with present-tense action verbs

Linking Verbs felt, is, am, seems, became, have, were, was

Editing and Proofreading Marks

∧	Add.
_❨_	Take out.
⬯⌒∧	Move to here.
∧	Add comma.
⊙	Add period.

Freedom Rider

At my school, we studies American history in fifth grade. Mr. Thompson are a great teacher. He sincere. Every day, he teach about heroes who important in the Civil Rights Movement. I a fan of Rosa Parks. She one of my heroes.

In 1955, buses in Montgomery, Alabama, were segregated. White people sat in the front, and African Americans sat in the back. If the bus full, African Americans had to give up their seats to white people. One night, though, Mrs. Parks especially tired. When her bus driver said to give her seat to a white person, she in her seat.

Mrs. Parks were an inspiration for others.

Grammar: Reteach

At the Beach

Grammar Rules Linking Verbs

A **linking verb** connects the **subject** of a sentence to a **word in the predicate** that describes or renames it.	The **beach** is Joe's favorite **place**.
• A **linking verb** can link the subject to an **adjective** or a **noun** in the predicate.	He **became** a good **swimmer** there.
• Common **linking verbs** are forms of *be, look, seem, feel, smell,* and *taste*.	He always **feels happy** at the beach.

Read each sentence. Circle the verb. If the verb is a linking verb, draw an arrow to connect the subject to a word in the predicate.

1. The water looks inviting.

2. Joe walks down to the water.

3. He studies the waves.

4. The waves seem high enough for body surfing.

5. Joe is ready to dive in!

   Describe your favorite place to a partner. Try to use linking verbs. Have your partner tell you which linking verbs you used.

Problems? Negotiate!

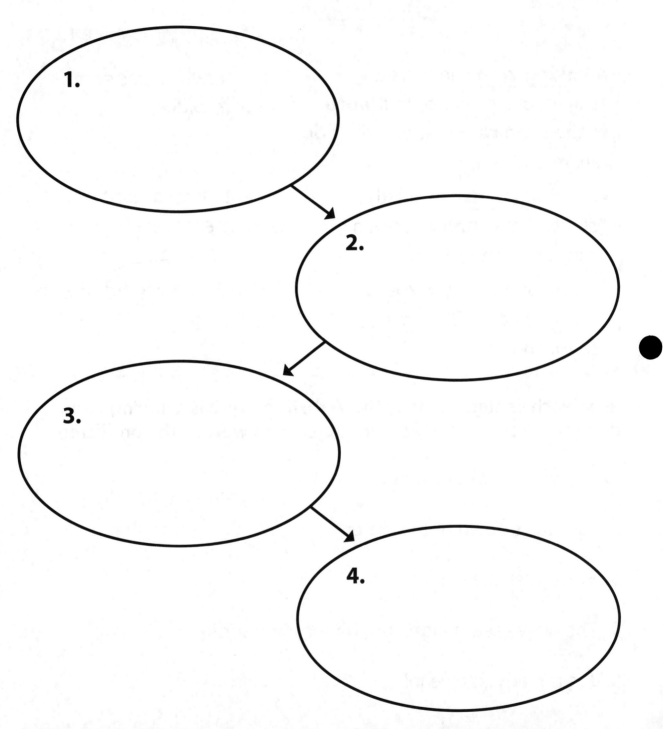

1.

2.

3.

4.

 Tell your partner about something you negotiated. Your partner writes the sequence of the negotiation in the sequence chain above.

Grammar: Game

What's the Topic?

Directions:

1. Team A starts. Player 1 spins the spinner and secretly notes the topic shown.

2. Player 1 uses a helping verb and an action verb to make a sentence about the topic.

3. Player 2 guesses what the topic is, based on Player 1's sentence. If Player 2 guesses correctly, the team gets one point. If Player 2 guesses incorrectly, Player 1 spins again and forms a second sentence about the topic. If he or she cannot guess correctly, the round is over.

4. Next, it is Team B's turn. Players 1 and 2 on Team B get two chances to score points as well.

5. Teams continue taking turns until one team scores five points.

Make a Spinner

1. Put a paper clip through the center of the circle.
2. Hold one end of the paper clip with a pencil.
3. Spin the paper clip around the pencil.

Grammar: Grammar and Writing

Edit and Proofread

Choose the Editing and Proofreading Marks you need to correct the passage. Make the following kinds of corrections:

- Add missing helping verbs.
- Use the present progressive tense.

Editing and Proofreading Marks

∧	Add.
ℐ	Take out.
⌐⊃ ∧	Move to here.
∧	Add comma.
⊙	Add period.

Rick's History Paper

Maria: Do you know what you ʌ*are* doing your history paper on?

Rick: I write about César Chávez. I think everyone know about him.

Maria: I reading about him, too. He helped migrant workers.

Rick: That's correct! He born into a family of farmers. He became a farm worker and fought against big landowners and companies.

Maria: I don't see how a worker fight a big landowner.

Rick: Chávez hoped workers join together to fight for their rights. He started a union that organize strikes. In the end, some agreements made between the workers and the landowners.

Maria: Good luck! I have looking forward to reading your paper.

Test-Taking Strategy Practice

Look for Important Words

Directions: Read each question about "Harvesting Hope." Choose the best answer.

Sample

1 What did César's family do after the drought of 1937?

Ⓒ His family moved to Arizona.

● His family moved to California.

Ⓔ His family moved to Mexico.

Ⓕ His family moved to Washington, DC.

2 How were migrant workers treated?

Ⓒ like children

Ⓓ like equals

Ⓔ like human beings

Ⓕ like slaves

3 What did César try to do before he organized the march?

Ⓒ He organized a strike.

Ⓓ He cut workers' pay.

Ⓔ He looked for another job.

Ⓕ He responded with violence.

 **Tell a partner how you used the strategy to answer the questions.**

Name _____ Date _____

"Harvesting Hope: The Story of César Chávez"

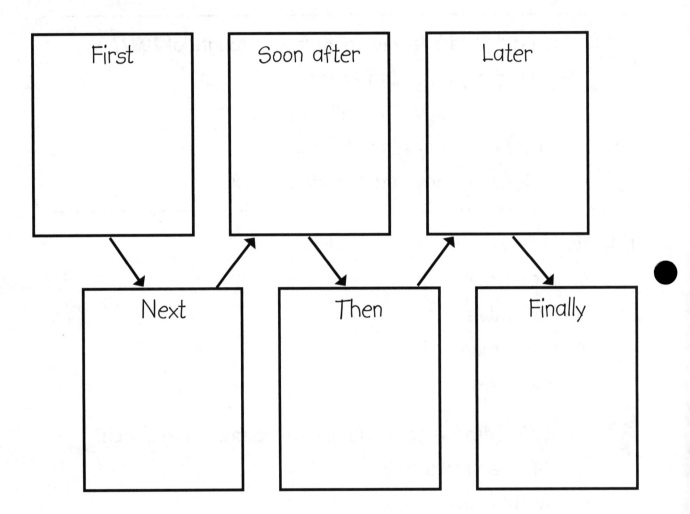

First

Soon after

Later

Next

Then

Finally

Use your sequence chain to retell the selection to a partner.

Fluency Practice

"Harvesting Hope: The Story of César Chávez"

Use this passage to practice reading with proper phrasing.

Until César Chávez was ten, every summer night was like a *fiesta*.   12

César and his brothers, sisters, and cousins settled down to sleep   24

outside, under netting to keep mosquitoes out. But who could sleep,   35

with uncles and aunts singing and telling tales of life back in Mexico?   48

César Chávez thought the whole world belonged to his family.   58

The eighty acres of their ranch were an island in the shimmering   70

Arizona desert, and the starry skies were all their own.   80

César's grandfather had built their large adobe house to last forever.   91

A vegetable garden, cows, and chickens supplied all the food they   102

could want. With hundreds of cousins on farms nearby, there was   113

always someone to play with.   118

Intonation

1 ☐ Rarely pauses while reading the text.   3 ☐ A Frequently pauses at appropriate points in the text.

2 ☐ Occasionally pauses while reading the text.   4 ☐ Consistently pauses at all appropriate points in the text.

Accuracy and Rate Formula

Use the formula to measure a reader's accuracy and rate while reading aloud.

_____ − _____ = _____

words attempted   number of errors   words correct per minute
in one minute   (wcpm)

Name _____ Date _____

Are We Going There?

Grammar Rules Helping and Present- Progressive Verbs

Helping verbs work with **main verbs**. They have different meanings: • *can* shows the ability to do something • *could, may,* and *might* show the possibility of something • *must, would,* and *should* show need, desire, or obligation	We **can** <u>plan</u> a vacation this year. We **might** <u>go</u> to the beach. We **should** <u>visit</u> the Grand Canyon this year.
A **present-progressive verb** tells about an action as it is happening. It uses **am, is** or **are** with a main verb that ends with **–ing**.	The family **is** <u>making</u> plans. Finally, we **are** <u>deciding</u>.

Choose a verb to complete each sentence. Use the correct forms.

1. Ana's family _____ visiting the Grand Canyon this summer.
(be, can)

2. The kids _____ pack their own bags.
(should, be)

3. Everyone _____ be surprised by what they see!
(might, can)

 Imagine you are going on a field trip. Tell a partner what you are planning to do. Use helping verbs.

Grammar: Game

Practice Makes Perfect

Directions:

1. Read question 1 below to your partner. (Be aware: It may have an error in the present-perfect tense, but don't fix it!)

2. Have your partner answer the question in writing, making any needed corrections in the present-perfect tense. The answer must be a sentence; it may not be simply "yes" or "no."

3. Award your partner one point if you agree that your partner's answer is correct and the present-perfect tense has been used correctly.

4. Next, your partner reads question 2 to you. Follow a similar procedure using steps 2 and 3 above.

5. Continue taking turns until all the questions have been answered correctly. Add up your points to see who is the winner.

Questions:

1. Have the filmmaker shown the injustices of the Sri Lankan war?

   _____

2. Has the women in the Iraqi police force protested?

   _____

3. Has the wars caused great injustice?

   _____

4. Have Roshini fought for women's rights?

   _____

5. Have they seen one of Roshini's films?

   _____

6. Has Roshini been a filmmaker for a long time?

   _____

Grammar: Game

I've Done That!

Directions:

1. Play this game with a partner. Work together to cut out the cards. Stack the cards face down, with the white cards in one pile and the gray cards in another.

2. Take turns. Draw one card from each stack. Form a sentence in present-perfect tense using the words on your cards. Use *has* or *have* plus the past participle of the verb on your white card. **Example: he, know:** He has known César Chávez for many years.

3. If you and your partner agree that your sentence is correct, you get one point. Then your partner takes a turn.

4. The first partner to reach five points wins. If both partners reach five points in the same turn, the game is a tie.

I	he	she
we	you	they
be	teach	know
begin	use	grow
do	have	go
visit	tell	say

Comparison Chart

Compare Literary Language

	"A Filmmaker for Justice"	"Harvesting Hope"
Similes	p. 281	p. 264 Every summer night was like
Metaphors	p. 284	p. 264 The eighty acres of their ranch were an island in the shimmering Arizona desert.
Imagery	p. 284 work for change	pp. 264–265 singing, happy,
Foreshadowing	p. 282	p. 269

Take turns with a partner. Make up a simile and a metaphor.

Grammar: Practice

Bus Strike

Grammar Rules Forms of *be* and *have*

1. For yourself, use *am* or *have*.

2. When you tell about another person or a thing, use *is* or *has*.

3. For yourself and one or more people, use *are* or *have*.

4. When you tell about other people and things, use *are* or *have*.

5. For linking verbs, use *am*, *is*, or *are* to link the subject to a word in the predicate.

6. For helping verbs, use *am*, *is*, or *are* with *-ing* verbs, and *has* or *have* with *-ed* verbs.

Write the correct forms of *be* and *have*. If a subject is also needed in the sentence, use a contraction.

A news reporter _____ just arrived at the bus headquarters.

Drivers _____ unhappy, and they _____ decided to strike.

The reporter interviewed the spokesperson for the drivers. She

asked, "Why _____ you protesting?"

The spokesperson replied, "We _____ all doing the same

job, but some drivers earn more than others. We _____ asked

for equal pay, but the officials _____ not agreed. So, _____

decided to strike until our demand for equal pay _____ met.

 Pick a form of *be* and a form of *have* and write two new sentences. Use a contraction in one of the sentences. Read your sentences to a partner.

Name _____   Date _____

Pioneer for Women's Rights by Frank Lee

In July 1920, Harry T. Burn, a state representative in Tennessee, cast the vote that passed the Nineteenth Amendment. The amendment gave women the right to vote in national elections. But the battle for this right began more than seventy years before—at a women's rights convention.

In 1848, Elizabeth Cady Stanton attended the Seneca Falls Convention, the first convention for women's rights in the United States. Stanton and others presented a document for women's rights, modeled after the Declaration of Independence. A key demand was the right to vote. With that right, women could change unfair laws such as the ones that limited their educational opportunities. The campaign for women's right to vote had started.

▲ Elizabeth Cady Stanton

Following the convention, Stanton combined her work to end slavery with achieving equal rights for women. Stanton believed that no human being should own or control another human being.

After the Civil War, Stanton increased her efforts for women's rights. She pushed for reforms that included the right to own property and to go to college. Stanton believed that women should be able to stand on their own.

In 1870, the Fifteenth Amendment gave the right to vote to African American men, but not to American women. Stanton was bitter over this setback, but she continued to fight for better social conditions and the vote for women until her death in 1902. With the passing of the amendment in 1920, women finally had a voice in their own government.

Mark-Up Reading

The Susan B. Anthony Amendment

by Judy Diaz

Susan B. Anthony was an activist by nature and worked for many causes. She was among many Americans who wanted to end slavery. She was also part of a far smaller group that wanted to improve the lives of American women. Women had many obstacles to gaining their rights.

▲ Susan B. Anthony

At the time, most women could not own property, weren't paid the same as men for the same labor, and could not vote. Anthony knew that with the right to vote, women would have the ability to change the laws. Achieving suffrage, or the right to vote, for women was the key. It became her lifelong goal, but its outcome would not be revealed until after her death.

When Anthony first started working for woman suffrage, she also faced obstacles. Too many people believed that women could not understand politics and were not smart enough to vote. The belief that women belonged at home was a huge barrier to getting the vote.

To help create a voice for women's rights, Anthony founded a newspaper called *The Revolution*. Its strong motto made her position clear: "Men, their rights, and nothing more; women, their rights, and nothing less." Anthony wanted women to have the same rights that men had.

After the Civil War, new amendments to the Constitution protected the rights of the newly freed slaves. The Fifteenth Amendment granted the right to vote to non-white citizens—including former slaves—but it applied only to males. Anthony wanted this amendment to apply to women too.

Mark-Up Reading

The Susan B. Anthony Amendment
(continued)

Anthony worked closely with Elizabeth Cady Stanton. Both agreed on how important it was for women to get the vote. But Anthony made the vote her only focus because she believed that voting was the best method Americans had for making changes in the nation. She dedicated her life to woman suffrage.

Anthony gathered petitions from 26 states with 10,000 signatures in support of women's right to vote, but Congress ignored her. She never gave up. Anthony continued to visit Congress annually to try and get them to revise the Fifteenth Amendment to include women. Despite continued efforts until her death in 1906, Anthony's attempts to change the amendment failed.

It wasn't until 1920 that her revision, later known as the "Susan B. Anthony" Amendment, was finally passed by Congress as the Nineteenth Amendment. Anthony did not live to see her goal achieved. But American women who can vote today are grateful for all of her hard work.

Compare the text structure of the two articles.

"Pioneer for Women's Rights"	Both	"The Susan B. Anthony Amendment"

Edit and Proofread

Choose the Editing and Proofreading Marks you need to correct the passage. Make the following kinds of corrections:

- Use present-perfect tense.
- Use the correct forms of *have* and *be*.

Editing and Proofreading Marks

∧	Add.
⨼	Take out.
⊂⊃∧	Move to here.
∧ (comma)	Add comma.
⊙	Add period.

Roshini Thinakaran ~~have~~ *has* used her filmmaking skills to show injustice. Her films has raised awareness of important social issues.

Roshini known injustice in her own life. She are from Sri Lanka, where a civil war made life harsh for her family. Roshini later studied journalism in college. Since then, her films told about women around the world who is working for justice.

Roshini have worked on a project about women who is living under oppression. Her stories has described women in Iraq, Liberia, Afghanistan, and other countries. She are hoping her films will help bring change to these countries.

Name _____ Date _____

Costa Rica

Grammar Rules Present-Perfect Tense

The **present-perfect tense** is formed by the present tense of **to have** + <u>a past</u> <u>participle</u>.	Jenny and Alex **have** <u>**visited**</u> Costa Rica many times with their family.
Most **past participles** end in **–ed**. • Some **past participles** are irregular. Here are a few: eat → eaten say → said see → seen take → taken teach → taught tell → told	Alex **has** <u>**wondered**</u> when they might go back. The people there **have** <u>**taught**</u> the family many amazing things.

Read the sentences. Rewrite the verbs in the present-perfect.

1. Jenny <u>sees</u> an active volcano. _____

2. Alex <u>visits</u> a cloud forest. _____

3. They <u>eat</u> churros in a café. _____

4. Their mom <u>takes</u> them snorkeling. _____

5. They <u>tell</u> us about their trip. _____

 Tell your partner about a place you have visited. Have your partner ask you questions. Use the present-perfect tense.

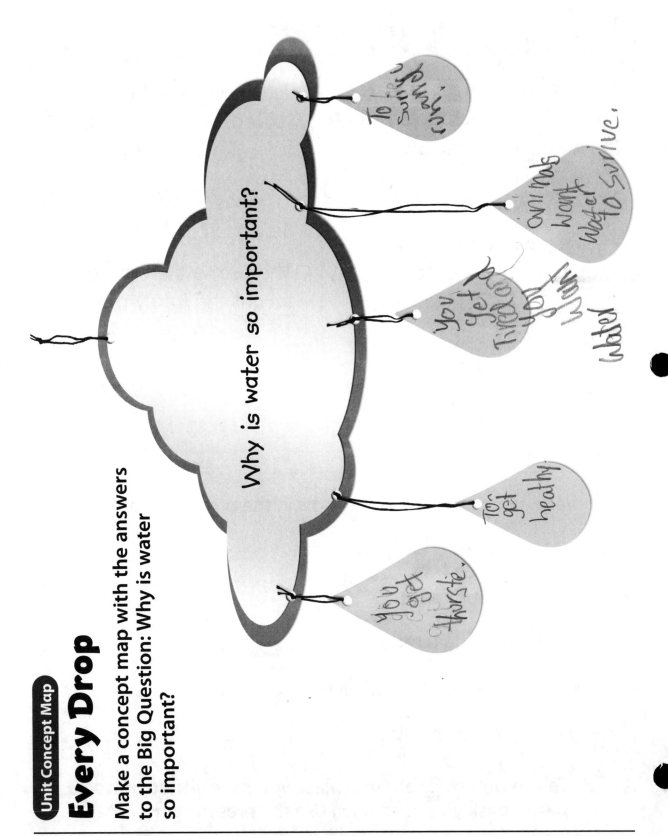

Unit Concept Map

Every Drop

Make a concept map with the answers to the Big Question: Why is water so important?

Why is water so important?

To plant flowers

animals want water to survive.

you get through your body water

To get healthy

you get thirsty.

Main Idea and Details

The Drought

I. _____

    A. _____

    B. _____

II. _____

    A. _____

    B. _____

III. _____

    A. _____

    B. _____

 Talk with a partner about ways water is important to Elena's family.

Grammar: Game

Point and Talk

This plant near us is growing well.

That truck over there is spraying water.

These rows of plants near us are growing well.

Those two trucks over there are spraying water.

Turn to page 318 in the Anthology, and use the sentences above to describe objects in the photo. Then play a game using more pictures in the book.

1. Team One holds the book, finds a picture, points to it, and describes something in the image using *this* or *these*.
2. Team Two points to the picture in Team One's hands and uses *that* or *those* to add more description.
3. Team Two takes the book, points to another picture, and describes the image using *this* or *these*.
4. Team One points to the picture in Team Two's hands and uses *that* or *those* to add more description.
5. Continue trading the book back and forth for three more rounds. Use *this* or *these* when your team has the book. Use *that* or *those* when the other team has the book.

Grammar: Grammar and Writing

Edit and Proofread

Choose the Editing and Proofreading Marks you need to correct the passage. Look for the following:

- correct placement of adjectives
- correct punctuation of two or more adjectives before a noun
- correct use of *this, that, these,* and *those*

Editing and Proofreading Marks

∧	Add.
✐	Take out.
⬭⤴∧	Move to here.
⋏	Add comma.
⊙	Add period.

A desert ⬭dry⬭ is. It is an area that receives precipitation little.

Animals that live in these hot dry places have special adaptations

that allow them to live without a constant supply of water. Camels

are one of this animals.

The interesting dromedary is. It is a camel with only hump one, but

it uses that hump very effectively. The camel can store up to 80 pounds

of fat in its hump. These fat can then be broken down into water

and energy for long treks across deserts without any water. Another

way camels conserve water is by not sweating, even in very hot

temperatures. This helps the camel go weeks several without water.

Name _____ Date _____

Reread

Directions: Read each question about "One Well." Choose the best answer.

Sample

> **1** What are animals mostly made of?
>
> Ⓐ muscles
>
> ● water
>
> Ⓒ air
>
> Ⓓ nests

2 What percent of fresh water do we have access to?

Ⓐ 3 percent

Ⓑ 97 percent

Ⓒ 1 percent

Ⓓ 99 percent

3 How does pollution in the atmosphere affect the water supply?

Ⓐ It can create acid rain.

Ⓑ It causes more rainfall.

Ⓒ It causes the water cycle.

Ⓓ It keeps water clean.

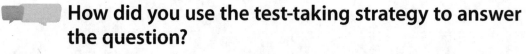 **How did you use the test-taking strategy to answer the question?**

Name _____ Date _____

"One Well"

I. All water on Earth is connected.

   A. about 70% of Earth's surface is water

   B. some water is buried deep under the ground

II. Water keeps moving through the water cycle.

   A. rises from water sources as gas or vapor

   B. Precipitation falls to earth

III. Plants + water depends on each other

   A. Transpiration - Water → vapor

   B. Water helps plants - photynthesis.

IV. Animal need water

   A. Water help the body do many things

   B. Animals are part of w.c

V. Watery homes

   A. Water is importing part of anim -als.

   B. Many animals depend entirely on watery places

VI. Access to the well.

   Population:

   A. Water has 20% of the water's

   B. Less water is available in Areas

💬 **Use Practice Master 5.7 to summarize "One Well."**

Fluency Practice

"One Well"

Use this passage to practice reading with proper phrasing.

Imagine for a moment that all the water on Earth came from just one   15
well. This isn't as strange as it sounds. All water on Earth is connected, so there   31
really *is* just one source, one global well, from which we can draw all our water.   48
Every ocean wave, every lake, stream, and underground river, every raindrop   60
and snowflake and every bit of ice in glaciers and polar icecaps is a part of this   76
global well.
                                                                             92

Because it is all connected, how we treat the water in the well will affect   102
every species on the planet, now and for years to come.

From "One Well," page 308.

Phrasing

1 ☐ Rarely pauses while reading the text.   3 ☐ Frequently pauses at appropriate points in the text.

2 ☐ Occasionally pauses while reading the text.   4 ☐ Consistently pauses at all appropriate points in the text.

Accuracy and Rate Formula
Use the formula to measure a reader's accuracy and rate while reading aloud.

_____ − _____ = _____
words attempted   number of errors   words correct per minute
in one minute   (wcpm)

Name _____ Date May 29 15

At the Zoo

Grammar Rules Adjectives

Adjectives describe what something is like. • Usually an **adjective** comes before a noun it tells about. • Use a **comma** to separate two or more adjectives before a **noun**.	The **graceful** giraffes eat the twigs on the trees. The **bright, colorful** parrots caw as we pass.
An **adjective** can also appear after a **linking verb** such as *is*, *are*, *look*, *feel*, *smell*, and *taste*.	The lion's mane <u>looks</u> fuzzy.
Demonstrative adjectives point out singular and plural nouns. • Use **this** and **these** to point out things nearby. • Use **that** and **those** to point out things far away.	**This** lion right in front of you is young. **Those** lions past the trees are older.

Circle the adjectives. Draw an arrow to the noun each adjective describes.

1. There is a long, curvy path through the zoo.

2. Did you see those monkeys in the tall trees?

3. This rhinoceros is huge.

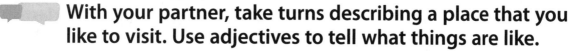 **With your partner, take turns describing a place that you like to visit. Use adjectives to tell what things are like.**

Grammar: Game

Adjective Bingo

Directions:

1. Cut out the cards and stack them facedown.

2. Take turns picking the top card and matching it with a square on the board.

3. Form a comparison adjective with the word and use it in a sentence.

4. If your partner agrees that your sentence is correct, place a marker on the word. If not, do not place a marker on the word.

5. The winner is the first player to have five markers in a row.

dry	shriveled	fresh	wet	important
fortunate	clean	beautiful	heavy	safe
watery	wise	**FREE**	fast	valuable
thin	difficult	late	wild	thirsty
tiny	confusing	windy	sad	busy

important	dry	heavy	clean	busy	tiny	late	wet
fresh	thirsty	confusing	fortunate	safe	fast	wild	thin
shriveled	beautiful	wise	difficult	valuable	watery	windy	sad

Toss and Describe

Directions:

1. Take turns tossing a marker onto one of the spaces.
2. Write a sentence that follows the directions in the space.
3. Play until every player has written five sentences.
4. Trade sentences with other players. Check each other's sentences. Give one point for each correct sentence.
5. The player with the most correct sentences wins.

Compare three or more things with a form of the word **wet**.	Compare with the word **most**.
Compare with the ending **-est**.	Compare with the word **least**.
Compare three things with a form of the word **large**.	Compare three things with a form of the word **cloudy**.
Compare with the word **most**.	Compare three or more things with a form of the word **windy**.
Compare three or more things with a form of the word **fresh**.	Compare three things with a form of the word **nice**.

Name _____ Date _____

Compare Texts

	"Picturing the Pantanal"	"One Well"
Genre		
Topic		
Main Idea	Using satellite images, Dr. Maycira Costa studies the Pantanal, and learns how life there is affected by changes to the area.	
Text Features	Photos: _____ Tables: _____ Diagrams: _____	Photos: _____ Tables: _____ Diagrams: _____

 Take turns with a partner. Share what you like about both selections. Share what you like that is in only one of the selections.

Grammar: Practice

The Pantanal

Grammar Rules Adjectives

1. Use a capital letter for adjectives that describe a country of origin.
2. Add **-er** to the adjective when you compare two things.
3. Add **-est** to the adjective to compare three or more things.
4. Some adjectives have special forms for comparing things. These include **good, better, best.**

Circle the adjectives. Underline the nouns they describe.

The Brazilian Pantanal is a strange and special place. It is the largest tropical wetland in the world. Many plants and animals live there. Heavy rain falls for months in the Pantanal. This makes the Pantanal green. It is much greener than the dry desert that Elena visited. Scientists want to learn about the amazing Pantanal. They study how human activities affect it. They believe this is the best way to protect the Pantanal for the future.

 Listen as a partner tells you a noun. Use an adjective to tell about that noun. Together, make a sentence that compares that noun to another noun.

Mark-Up Reading

Why Save the Wetlands? by Dinah Garton

Wetlands have many names—marshes, bogs, swamps—but perhaps we should just call them important! For example, wetlands help nearby communities by storing fresh water. Just one acre of wetland holds 1 to 1.5 million gallons of fresh water! In this way, wetlands help prevent water shortages. Also, when rivers overflow, wetlands absorb and store the extra, fast-moving water. Then they release it slowly back into the environment. This helps reduce the risk of flooding and keeps communities dry.

▲ Wetlands are an important—and beautiful—ecosystem.

Wetlands also benefit communities by filtering water, removing dirt and other solids from it. When polluted runoff from cities flows into the wetlands, the dense plant growth slows it down. Because the water is moving slowly, some of the dirt and pollutants settle on the wetland floor. Microorganisms in the soil then break down some of these pollutants to make them less harmful. This process helps to remove both dirt and pollutants from the water.

At the same time, plants absorb extra nutrients in the water. Removing these nutrients helps the plants to grow and cleans the water. Because of the filtering process, water that flows out of wetlands is much cleaner.

Explanation: _____

_____

_____

_____

_____

Why Save the Wetlands? (continued)

Despite their many benefits, people have been slow to recognize the importance of wetlands. Wetlands are in trouble, and human activities such as industry, construction, and farming are to blame. Agriculture is a leading cause of wetland destruction. When land is cleared for farmland, wetlands are often drained. Canals and ditches used for irrigation also damage wetlands. When water is diverted into a canal, it increases the speed of water flowing into and through the wetland. Because a wetland uses the slow release of water to absorb and filter water, the wetland's ability to do this is affected.

▲ Too much pollution can overwhelm a wetland.

Explanation: _____
_____
_____
_____

Fewer than half the nation's original wetlands remain. The loss of wetlands means losing all of the benefits that they bring. Without wetlands, watersheds become more polluted, water shortages become more frequent, and the risk of flooding increases. Protecting our remaining wetlands is the first step. Educating people about the importance of wetlands can help to protect them and hopefully, change actions that harm them. As a result, people may realize why we need to save them.

Grammar: Grammar and Writing

Edit and Proofread

Choose the Editing and Proofreading Marks you need to correct the passage. Look for the following:

- correct use and spelling of comparison adjectives
- correct capitalization of proper adjectives
- correct use of irregular comparison adjectives

Editing and Proofreading Marks

∧	Add.
ℐ	Take out.
⌒∧	Move to here.
≡	Capitalize.
⊙	Add period.

Our class just read about the most excitingest litter campaign. It's

called "Skip the Bag, Save the River." It is aimed at one of the most big

problems facing american rivers: plastic bags. A new law was passed

in Washington, DC, that is more effectiver than the old law. People

there now have to pay an additional five cents for any plastic bags they

get for food and carryout. The money raised from these fees goes to

making the Anacostia River more clean than it's been in years.

Our class feels that this law is a really gooder idea. But we have an

even goodest idea. We are going to take the No Plastic Pledge. This

means that we will stop using and buying plastics. I think that plastic is

one of our most concerningest environmental problems.

Grammar: Reteach

Camping Out

Grammar Rules Adjectives

• To compare two things, add **-er** to the adjective. Often you'll use the word **than**, too. • For longer adjectives, do not use **-er**. Use **more** or **less**.	Molly and I pitch a **big** tent. Dad pitches a **bigger** tent **than** ours. Our campsite is **more beautiful than** our neighbors'.
• To compare more than two things, add **-est**. Use **the** before the adjective. • For longer adjectives, do not use **-est**. Use **most** or **least**.	They pitch **the biggest** tent of all. Our spot is **the most beautiful** of all.
Some adjectives such as **good, better**, and **best**, have special forms for comparing.	Friday's lunch was **good**. Saturday's lunch was **better**. **The best** lunch was on Sunday.

Choose the correct adjective to complete each sentence.

1. We hike up _____ hill.
(the highest, higher)

2. I am tired, but Dad is _____.
(the most tired, more tired)

3. The view from the hilltop is _____
(more beautiful than, most beautiful)

the view from our campground!

4. Everyone had _____ time!
(the best, better)

With your partner, compare classroom objects.

Name _____ Date _____

Characters My Partner Knows

Character	Role	Function	Relationship

 Use your chart to describe characters in a story your partner tells you about.

Grammar: Game

Spin and Speak

Directions:

1. Play with a partner. Take turns spinning the spinner. Follow the directions in the space you land on. Use the word in a sentence.

2. If your partner agrees that the sentence is correct, give yourself a point.

3. Play until both of you have spun four times. Who has more points?

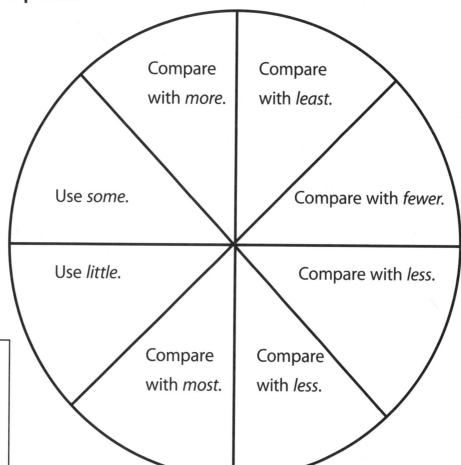

Make a Spinner

1. Place one loop of a paper clip over the center of the circle.
2. Push a sharp pencil through the loop and the paper.
3. Spin the paper clip around the pencil.

Grammar: Grammar and Writing

Edit and Proofread

Choose the Editing and Proofreading Marks you need to correct the passage. Look for the following:

- correct capitalization of proper adjectives
- correct use of comparison adjectives
- correct use of irregular comparison adjectives

Editing and Proofreading Marks

∧	Add.
ℒ	Take out.
⊂⊃∧	Move to here.
≡	Capitalize.
⊙	Add period.

Last summer, I went out West with my family. The ~~goodest~~ *best* thing I

saw on the trip was the Hoover Dam. This dam was built on the arizona-

nevada border in the 1930s. It took about five years to build. That's most

time than it took to build the Empire State Building. And it's no wonder!

It has some concrete than any other structure I've seen. The dam

created Lake Mead, which is the one of the bestest centers of outdoor

recreation in the whole area. At the base of the dam is a power plant.

Some than half of the power generated goes to Southern california

cities. The rest goes to Arizona and Nevada. Even though the Hoover

Dam is a tourist attraction, less people visit it than the Grand Canyon.

That's a real shame because the dam is an amazing american wonder!

Test-Taking Strategy Practice

Reread

Directions: Read each question and choose the best answer.

Sample

Fatima's village used camels to pull water for drinking and washing and cooking. The people rely on the trees to get through the dry season. In Sudan, the climate is very hot and dry. Rain only comes during the rainy seasons.

1 Why do you think Fatima's village decides to get a pump?

- Ⓐ The camels can no longer be used.
- Ⓑ The trees are dying.
- Ⓒ The area gets plenty of rain.
- ● The village needs water in this dry and hot climate.

2 Why will a pump make life easier for Fatima's village?

- Ⓐ The pump will help the people fill the trees with water.
- Ⓑ They will no longer have to use camels or trees to get water.
- Ⓒ It will give the camels a large supply of food.
- Ⓓ People will dance with their friends and celebrate the new pump.

3 Grandmother still prepares her tree for the rainy season. Why does she do this?

- Ⓐ The climate is hot and dry.
- Ⓑ The camels need water.
- Ⓒ The trees need water.
- Ⓓ The people want to celebrate.

How did you use the test-taking strategy to answer the question?

Character Chart

"My Great-Grandmother's Gourd"

Character	Role	Function	Relationship
Grandmother	grandmother		
Fatima	granddaughter		

Use your character chart to retell the story to a partner.

Fluency Practice

"My Great-Grandmother's Gourd"

Use this passage to practice reading with proper expression.

I looked for my grandmother, who always says she is so proud	12
of me, but I didn't see her. As people pushed forward to try the	26
pump, I pushed outward to find my grandmother.	34
There she stood all alone beneath her best friend, an old	45
baobab tree.	47
"Grandmother, come see the new pump. The water is so easy to	59
get now, our work will be less."	66
Grandmother looked at me, then patted the gnarled trunk of the	77
giant baobab tree with her work-worn hand and said, "Go child.	88
Drink the fresh, cold water. And soon I'll be there too."	99
I ran back and danced with my friends, celebrating the new	110
pump. But my grandmother did not come.	117

From "My Great-Grandmother's Gourd," page 344.

Expression

[1] ☐	Does not read with feeling.		[3] ☐	Reads with appropriate feeling for most content.
[2] ☐	Reads with some feeling, but does not match content.		[4] ☐	Reads with appropriate feeling for all content.

Accuracy and Rate Formula
Use the formula to measure a reader's accuracy and rate while reading aloud.

$$\underline{} \quad - \quad \underline{} \quad = \quad \underline{}$$

words attempted in one minute	number of errors	words correct per minute (wcpm)

Name _____ Date _____

Where Shall We Go?

Grammar Rules Adjectives

• Use a **capital letter** for a **proper adjective**. • Use a **capital letter** for any **proper noun** used as an adjective.	Lake Erie is in America. It is an <u>**American**</u> lake. What are some other <u>Illinois</u> lakes?
• Some adjectives have special forms for comparing things, such as **more/most**. • To compare amounts, use **less/least**. • To compare things that can be counted, use **fewer/fewest**.	There are **more** clouds today than yesterday. There is **less** rain today than yesterday. Mom counted the **fewest** birds on Friday.

Write the correct form of the words to complete each sentence.

1. Lake Tahoe is another _____ lake.
          (american)

2. It is a popular skiing destination for _____ residents.
                                                      (california)

3. This winter, there is already _____ snow there.
                                          (some/most)

4. But this year's snowfall is _____ than last year's.
                                       (less/least)

5. Two years ago, the resort had the _____ number of skiers.
                                              (least/fewest)

 Tell a partner about two or more activities you like to do. Use adjectives to describe how you feel about them.

Grammar: Game

Choose and Write

Directions:

1. Take turns choosing a box. Make sure no one else has initialed it.

2. Read the noun in the box. Write the possessive form on the line.

3. Use the possessive noun in an oral sentence.

4. Have the other players check your work. If they agree that your possessive noun is correct, write your initials in the box.

5. When all the boxes are initialed, count your boxes. The player with the most boxes wins.

girl	Thomas	water	pump	gourd
____	____	____	____	____
Elena	cross	canal	rancher	rain
____	____	____	____	____
story	class	Timmy	Sally	cup
____	____	____	____	____
Lou	village	bus	forest	canyon
____	____	____	____	____
man	Ross	Taylor	family	river
____	____	____	____	____
mountain	Peter	valley	boy	hill
____	____	____	____	____

Grammar: Game

The Make-It-Possessive Game

Grammar Rules Singular and Plural Possessives		
One Owner	Add **'s**.	A village's water is for everyone.
More Than One Owner	Add **'** if the noun ends in **-s**.	The villagers' resources are important.

Directions:

1. Play with a partner. Flip a coin. Move one space for heads, two spaces for tails.

2. Change the noun to a possessive and write a sentence using it. If your partner agrees that your sentence is correct, stay on the space. If not, go back one space.

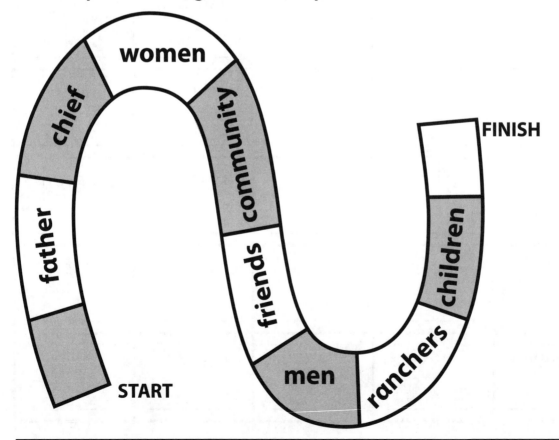

Name _____ Date _____

Compare Themes

Themes	"Juan del Oso and the Water of Life"	"My Great-Grandmother's Gourd"
Many hands make light work.	Yes	
Work that has a purpose can benefit many.		Yes
With hard work, anything is possible.		
Don't give up old ways for new ways.		
Water is important to our lives.		
Teamwork works.		

 Take turns with a partner giving examples from the selection to support your answers.

Grammar: Practice

The Aquifer's Future

Grammar Rules Possessive Nouns and Adjectives

1. When there is only one owner, add **'s** to show ownership.

2. When there is more than one owner and the noun ends in **-s**, just add **'** at the end of the noun.

3. When there is more than one owner and the noun does not end in **-s**, add **'s** at the end of the noun.

4. Possessive adjectives are **my, your, her, his, its, our**, and **their**.

5. Remember not to use an apostrophe with possessive adjectives.

Directions:

1. Write the correct endings for possessive nouns.

2. Write possessive adjectives.

All of the town _____ citizens gathered at town hall, anxious to hear _____ mayor speak. _____ speech would be the most important she had ever made. News reporters _____ cameras were ready to film. She cleared her voice and began.

"We've had a severe drought this summer and the aquifer in _____ region is drying up. Each community in the region must begin _____ own water-saving policy. It is _____ proposal that we begin water rationing immediately. We must save every drop of water we can now to ensure _____ availability in the future. _____ lives depend on it!"

 Write two new sentences using a possessive noun and a possessive adjective. Discuss your sentences with a partner.

Mark-Up Reading

The Giant Cloud-Swallower

A Zuñi legend retold by Georgia Byrne

Long ago, a giant named Cloud-Swallower lived on the cliffs, greedily gulping down any cloud that floated over the canyon. Without clouds, there was no rain, and the region was bone dry. "We need water!" cried the people.

Many went alone to slay the giant, but none returned. Then one day, Mátsailéma said to his twin, Áhaiyúta, "No one alone has been able to defeat the giant. To slay him, we must try a new strategy, so let us go together."

Áhaiyúta agreed, adding, "We should ask wise Spider for help, too."

"I know what to do," said Spider, and as Cloud-Swallower dozed, she wove a thick web across his eyes.

As the twins approached, Cloud-Swallower heard them and woke, thundering, "Have you come to slay me?" Jumping to his feet, he realized he was blinded. He whirled wildly, shouting, "Where are you?"

"We are here!" called Áhaiyúta, from the cliff's edge. Cloud-Swallower charged him, but Áhaiyúta dodged, leaving Cloud-Swallower teetering on the edge. Mátsailéma gave the giant brute a great shove, and Cloud-Swallower tumbled into the abyss below, defeated.

"Our people thank you for your assistance," the brothers said to Spider. "Now the rains will fall freely!"

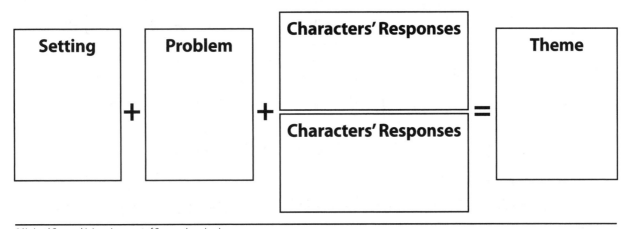

Setting		Problem		Characters' Responses		Theme
	+		+		=	
				Characters' Responses		

Mark-Up Reading

A Legend of the Great Flood

An Australian Aboriginal legend retold by W.J.Thomas

A terrible drought swept across the plains. All the water had left the creeks and water holes. Clouds no longer drifted across the hills.

All the animals met to discover the cause of the drought. When they arrived at the meeting place, they discovered that an enormous frog had swallowed all the water in the land. It was decided that the only way to obtain water again was to make the frog laugh. After much argument, the Kookaburra was chosen to be first to try.

The animals formed a circle around the frog. The Kookaburra began to laugh, louder and louder. The other animals looked on, but the frog seemed to sleep. The Kookaburra laughed until he nearly choked, but with no success.

The next competitor was a frill-lizard, who extended the frill around his throat and puffed out his jaws. The frog didn't even notice him.

Finally, a huge eel suggested that he should try. Many of the animals laughed at this, but they finally agreed. So the eel began to wriggle, slowly first, and then faster and faster. He slowed down and shook his body. Then he flopped about like a grub on an anthill.

The frog opened his eyes, his body quivered, and he burst into a laugh like rolling thunder. Water poured from his mouth in a flood, covering the land. Gradually the flood subsided, and the land was once again green.

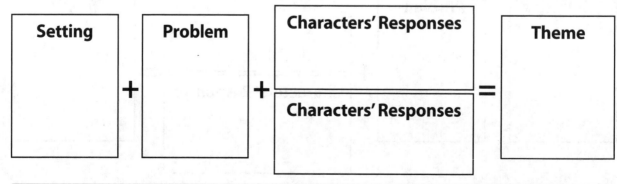

Setting		Problem		Characters' Responses		Theme
	+		+		=	
				Characters' Responses		

Grammar: Grammar and Writing

Edit and Proofread

Choose the Editing and Proofreading Marks you need to correct the passage. Look for the following:

- correct punctuation and spelling of possessive nouns and adjectives
- whether the possessive adjective matches the number of owners

Editing and Proofreading Marks

∧	Add.
ℐ	Take out.
∨̇	Add apostrophe (').
⊙	Add period.

Pecos Bill could ride anything. Bills skill was well-known all over the West. Bill got thrown only once in their career. It was when he decided to ride a tornado. Now Bill was picky. He wasn't going to ride your average Joes tornado. Bill waited for the fiercest tornado ever. It's roaring was so loud it woke up people in France.

Well, Bill just grabbed that tornado and jumped on it's back. The tornado spun all the way to the Rio Grande. It tied Texas' rivers into knots and flattened Oklahomas forests. But Bill calmly rode along, jabbing the tornado occasionally with her spurs.

Finally, that tornado' energy was gone. So it rained itself out. It rained so much that it created the Grand Canyon. That tornado was down to nothing when Bill fell off at last.

Name _____ Date _____

A Show for the Birds

Grammar Rules Possessives

A **possessive noun** tells who owns something. • For one owner, add -**'s**. • For more than one owner, add an apostrophe (**'**) to the plural noun. • For plural nouns with special forms, add -**'s** to the plural noun.	The bird**'s** nest is new. The three bird**s'** nests are new. The children**s'** pets are ready to perform.
A **possessive adjective** replaces an owner's name. • It does *not* use an apostrophe. • If there is one owner, use: **my, your, his, her, its.** • If there is more than one owner, use: **our, your, their**	Nara has a bird. **Her** bird is a canary. Nara and Mina's bird is blue. **Their** bird is a parrot.

Write the word that correctly completes each sentence.

1. The _____ give _____ family a lot of laughs.
        (birds/bird's)   (our/our's)

2. _____ bird is funny as it plays _____ bell.
    (Your/Your's)   (its/it's/its')

3. Let's have a talent show with all the _____ pets!
                                        (people/peoples')

4. If Tim has _____ parrot, the _____ act will win.
            (his/his')   (parrots/parrot's)

  Describe a pet you know. Use possessive nouns and adjectives.

Unit Concept Map

The Wild West

Make a concept map with the answers to the Big Question:
What does it take to settle a new land?

What does it take to settle a new land?

Name _____ Date _____

Identify Causes and Effects

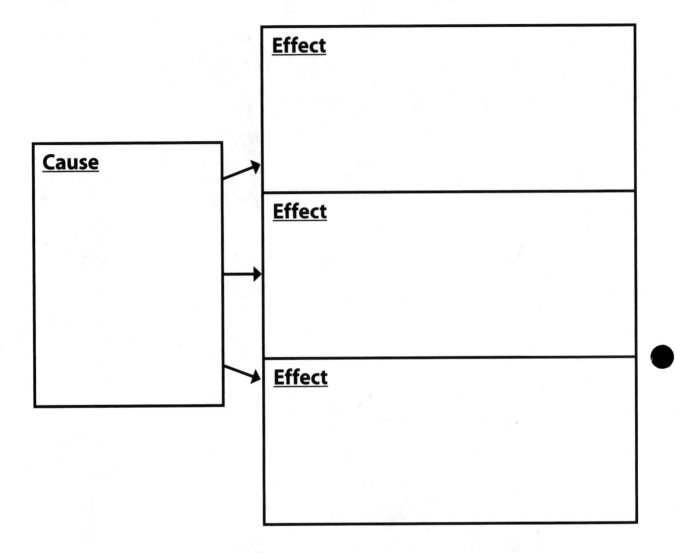

Tell your partner which effect you find most interesting and why.

Grammar: Game

Spin and Speak

Directions:

1. Make up a sentence for the object pronoun selected.

2. If the other players agree that you used the pronoun correctly, give yourself one point.

3. The first player to get 5 points is the winner.

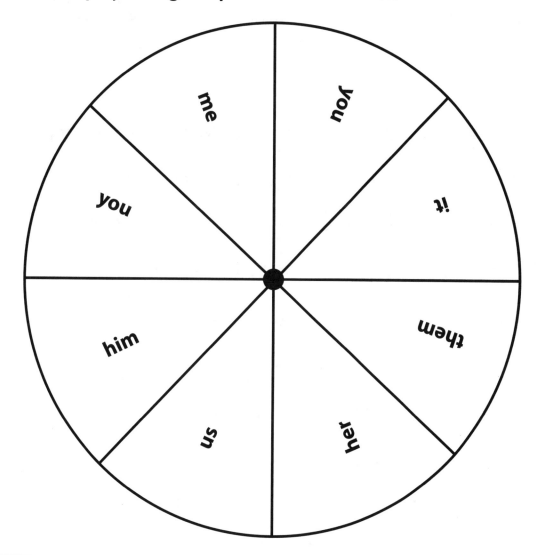

Make a Spinner

1. Place one loop of a paper clip over the center of the circle.
2. Push a sharp pencil through the loop and the paper.
3. Spin the paper clip around the pencil.

Grammar: Grammar and Writing

Edit and Proofread

Choose the Editing and Proofreading Marks you need to correct the passage. Look for the following:

- correct use of subject and object pronouns
- use of the pronoun *it* without an antecedent

Editing and Proofreading Marks

∧	Add.
ℐ	Take out.

I
~~me~~ wanted to know what being a cowboy was like. My sister
     ∧
Nikki and me got the chance last summer. Mom took Nikki and I to a

working cattle ranch that lets tourists stay and work for a week. They

is the only place where you pay to work. Us stayed in bunkhouses.

Was hot there. The bunkhouses had no air conditioning.

The best part was having my own horse. His name was Jacks. She

was brown with a white streak on his nose. Different cowboys taught

us different things. Them were really patient with us. Mitch taught

we how to wrangle cattle. Nikki was much better at it than I was. Her

could make her horse do anything. Mary taught us how to lasso. Now I

can lasso Nikki anytime her annoys me.

Test-Taking Strategy Practice

Predict the Answer

Directions: Read each question about "Westward Bound!" Choose the best answer.

Sample

1 Sod houses built around rooms carved out of a hillside were called _____ .

Ⓐ settlements

Ⓑ explorations

Ⓒ territories

● dugouts

2 Around what year did people start moving to the West in large numbers?

Ⓐ 1705

Ⓑ 1790

Ⓒ 1988

Ⓓ 1803

3 Why did settlers mostly go west?

Ⓐ to meet English, Scottish, and French fur traders

Ⓑ to start plantations

Ⓒ to find land

Ⓓ to find big cities

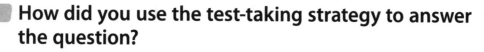 **How did you use the test-taking strategy to answer the question?**

Cause-and-Effect Organizer

"Westward Bound!"

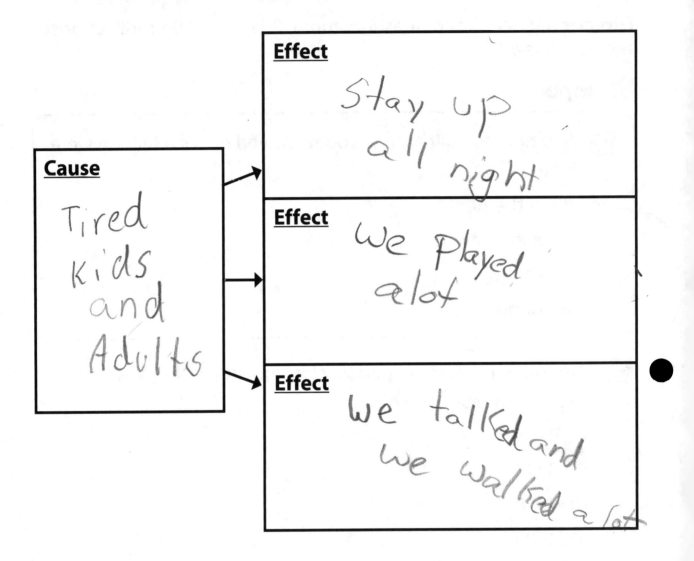

Cause

Tired kids and Adults

Effect

Stay up all night

Effect

We Played alot

Effect

we talked and we walked a lot

Use your organizer to retell the selection to a partner.

Fluency Practice

"Westward Bound!"

Use this passage to practice reading with proper intonation.

If you ask anyone about the history of the West, they may tell you about a wild,   17

lawless time, when brave cowboys rode their horses across wide, dusty plains.   29

This is a popular vision of the Old West. It is often shown on TV and in the   47

movies. But it is not the whole story.   55

The real history of the West is much more interesting. It is the story of millions   71

of different kinds of people, all with different ideas about the land and their   85

future on it. They came from many different backgrounds, but they had one   98

thing in common. They lived in a time of great changes. It was the time of the   115

westward expansion.   117

From "Westward Bound!", page 386.

Intonation

| 1 | ☐ Does not change pitch. | 3 | ☐ Changes pitch to match some of the content. |
| 2 | ☐ Changes pitch, but does not match content. | 4 | ☐ Changes pitch to match all of the content. |

Accuracy and Rate Formula

Use the formula to measure a reader's accuracy and rate while reading aloud.

$$\underline{\hspace{3cm}} \quad - \quad \underline{\hspace{3cm}} \quad = \quad \underline{\hspace{3cm}}$$

words attempted   number of errors   words correct per minute
in one minute   (wcpm)

Around the Neighborhood

Grammar Rules Pronouns

Subject pronouns must agree in number and gender with their **antecedents**. • The **pronoun** *it* can be a subject with or without an **antecedent**.	<u>Liz</u> likes to shop. **She** shops for fruit. <u>The market</u> is busy. **It** is noisy. **It** is time to shop.
Object pronouns agree in number and gender with their **antecedents**. • **Object pronouns** come after **verbs** or small words such as *to*, *for*, or *of*.	The baker bakes <u>muffins</u>. He **bakes them** for us. I go to the <u>market</u>. I go **to it** every week.

Read each sentence. Circle the correct subject or object pronoun.

1. Liz smiles as we walk by. We wave to (she, her).

2. My sister and I missed the bus! (We, Us) walk to school.

3. Mrs. Potter loves her flower garden. (She, Her) is a great gardener.

4. Mr. Hernandez helps his students. He helps (us, we) to understand.

5. The students are quiet. (It, Them) is time to study!

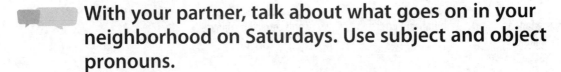 **With your partner, talk about what goes on in your neighborhood on Saturdays. Use subject and object pronouns.**

Grammar: Game

Pronoun Concentration

Directions:

1. Cut out the cards. Place them face down on the playing area.

2. Take turns turning over two cards.

3. If your cards have a subject pronoun that matches its reflexive form, use the words in a sentence. If the other players agree that your sentence is correct, keep the cards.

4. If your cards do not match, return them to the playing area.

5. Play until all the pronouns have been matched. The player with the most matches wins.

he	we	I	you
she	it	you	they
themselves	itself	ourselves	yourself
myself	himself	yourselves	herself

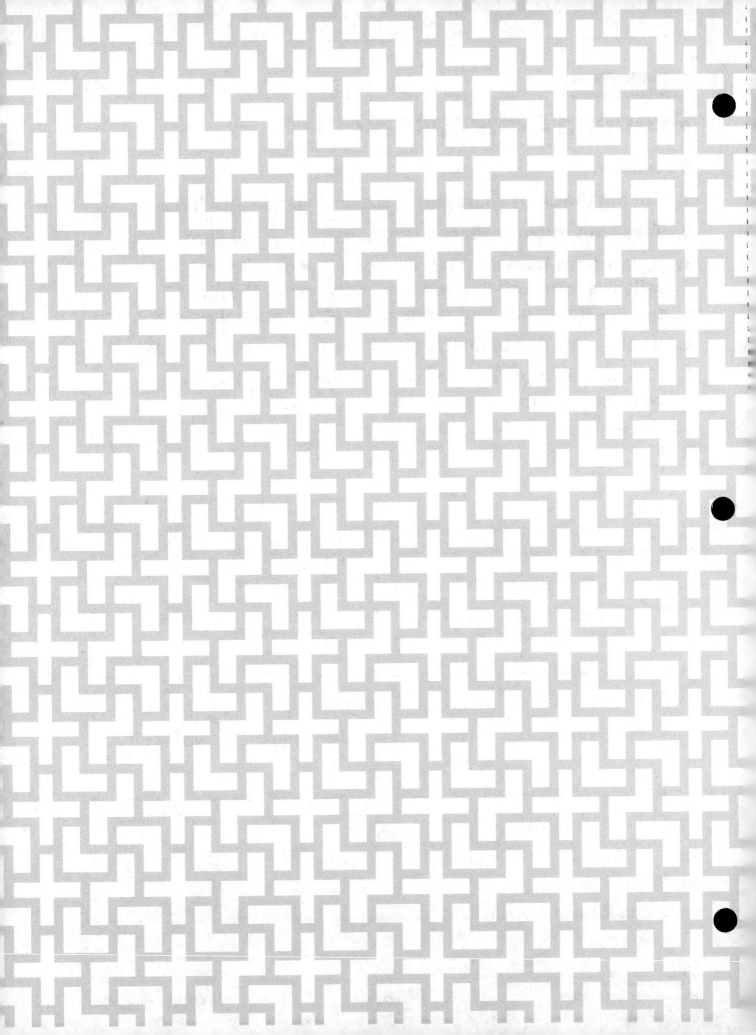

Grammar: Game

Reflexive Pronoun Challenge

Directions:

1. Set a timer for one minute.
2. Circle the reflexive pronoun in each sentence, and draw an arrow to its antecedent.
3. Stop your work after one minute.
4. Trade papers with a partner and check each other's work.
5. The one with more correct answers is the winner.

---

1. Cowboys often wore bandanas to protect themselves from dust.

2. The bandana itself could also be used as a washcloth or a bandage.

3. One cowboy said, "I don't know how I'd safeguard myself without my bandana.

4. Another cowboy said, "We also need broad-brimmed hats to protect ourselves from the sun."

5. A cowgirl also needed a hat to protect herself from the sun, but hers was usually more fashionable.

6. The sign outside the general store read, "Cowboys! Prepare yourselves for the cattle drive ahead. Get your supplies here!"

7. A cowboy also needed to wear chaps to protect himself from horns and sagebrush.

8. A wise old cowboy advised, "You should always have a song in your heart to keep yourself from getting lonely."

Name _____ Date _____

Compare Authors' Purposes

	"A Day in the Life of a Vaquero"	"Westward Bound!"
What was the author's main purpose? • give information or explain • persuade readers • entertain, describe, or express personal feelings • tell how to do something		
How do you know? Give examples.		

 Take turns with a partner. Share one question you could ask both authors. Share one question you have for only one author.

Grammar: Prounoun Agreement

Lewis and Clark

Circle the nouns. Rewrite the sentence with pronouns in place of the nouns.

Grammar Rules Pronoun Agreement

1. Use **I** or **me** to talk about yourself. Use **we** or **us** to talk about yourself and another person.

2. Use **he** or **him** for a boy or man. Use **she** or **her** for a girl or woman. Use **it** for a thing.

3. Use **they** or **them** for two or more people or things. Use **you** to talk to one person or more than one person.

4. Use pairs of pronouns that match in person and number to talk about a person twice in one sentence. (he, himself)

1. Sacajawea helped Lewis and Clark. _____

2. Lewis and Clark asked questions. _____

3. President Jefferson learned a lot because of Sacajawea, too.

   _____

4. Lewis and Clark were great. _____

5. Now President Jefferson, the people, and I know a lot about the American West. _____

> **Have a partner choose a noun. Tell the noun's number and gender. Then pick a pronoun that can replace the noun. Together, make a sentence using a pair of pronouns with that number and gender.**

Mark-Up Reading

Adapted from

ONE MAN'S GOLD
BY ENOS CHRISTMAN

Friday, May 25, 1851

One who has not been in California can hardly credit the changes that take place here in a very short period of time. Just one short year ago, I was crossing the barren plains on foot. Back then, a gold hunter had to carry everything he required with him. Often I have footed it a distance of fifteen or twenty miles over a burning, dusty plain without being able to get a drop of water unless I carried it with me. Now everything here is different. No canteen is needed. You need not carry your blankets. All along the roads, trading tents and good houses are erected. Travelers can find good meals as well as a good, clean bed.

Explanation: _____

_____

_____

_____

Name _____   Date _____

A Letter Home

BY EDMUND BOOTH *Adapted from personal letters*

Nov. 3, 1850

My Dear Wife,

Probably you are thinking that I am now on my way home, and so I expected to be. Alas! I am in California for another winter.

[Several weeks ago] a man offered me a half share in a damming company on condition that I worked until the dam was finished. After two weeks of the most laborious work I ever performed, we had a rain which must have been very heavy in the higher mountains. On the next day, every dam on the river, including our own, was either destroyed or greatly injured.

It was a most bitter disappointment all along. We had all expected to make our thousands and go home this Autumn.

Your affectionate husband,
Edmund

Explanation: _____

_____

_____

_____

Mark-Up Reading

EL DORADO, 1849

BY LUZENA STANLEY WILSON *Adapted from oral history*

From the brow of a steep mountain we [my family and I] caught the first glimpse of a mining camp. Nevada City, a row of canvas tents lining each of the two ravines, lay at our feet.

We were not rich enough for the luxury of a canvas home. So, a few pine boughs and branches of the undergrowth were cut and thrown into a rude shelter for the present. Since our experience with rain [flooding] in Sacramento, we thought that rain was one of the daily or at least weekly occurrences of a California spring. As a result, the first precaution was to secure a water-tight shelter. Our bedding was placed inside the little brush house. My cook stove was set up near it under the shade of a great pine tree. Thus, I was established, without further preparation, in my new home. When I was left alone in the afternoon, I tried to think of ways to increase our low family finances. I thought of taking boarders. There was already a thriving establishment of the kind just down the road. Under the shelter of a canvas roof, its sign read: "Wamac's Hotel. Meals $1.00."

Explanation: _____

_____

_____

_____

_____

_____

_____

Mark-Up Reading

EL DORADO, 1849 (continued)

I decided to set up a rival hotel, but I needed to build it first. So I bought two boards from a precious pile belonging to a man who was building the second wooden house in town. All by myself I chopped stakes and drove them into the ground. Then I set up my table and bought supplies at a neighboring store. When my husband came back at night he found twenty miners eating at my

table. Because they liked what they ate, every man put a dollar in my hand and said I might count him as a permanent customer. Since I believed my hotel would bring me gold, I called it "El Dorado."

Explanation: _____
_____
_____
_____

From the first day, it was well visited. The miners were glad to get something to eat. In six weeks we had saved money enough to pay the man who brought us up from Sacramento. In a little time, the frame of a house grew up around me, and presently my cook stove and brush house were enclosed under a roof.

Explanation: _____
_____

Grammar: Grammar and Writing

Edit and Proofread

Choose the Editing and Proofreading Marks you need to correct the passage. Look for the following:

- correct use of subject, object, and reflexive pronouns.

Editing and Proofreading Marks

∧	Add.
℘	Take out.

The dry goods store was going out of business. Mrs. Colter looked

around. "Are you folks closing the store ~~himself~~ *yourselves*?" she asked Stitch.

Stitch replied, "You can see for yourselves that there are no

customers. They have all left to get himself new jobs."

"My husband and me aren't leaving," sniffed Mrs. Colter. "Him and

I still have customers."

"People have to eat," said the owner. "Your husband's got herself

a good little business with that grocery store."

"We've worked myself to the bone, feeding people in this town,"

exclaimed Mrs. Colter. "Them can't leave just because the mine has

run themselves dry!"

"Me agree," replied Stitch. "But I have a family to feed. I have to

move where people have the money to buy my goods."

Name _____ Date _____

Band Practice

Grammar Rules Reflexive Pronouns

A **reflexive pronoun** acts as an object and refers back to the subject.	Rose taught **herself** the guitar.
• Singular **reflexive pronouns** end with **-self**.	Mark chose the songs by **himself**.
• Plural **reflexive pronouns** end with **-selves**.	Mark, Rose, and I formed the band **ourselves**.

Use reflexive pronouns to complete the sentences.

1. Mark hums the new songs to _____.

2. Rose sings to _____, too, so she can get the tune right.

3. Rose and Brett ask _____ if they're ready for a duet.

4. Brett doesn't like performing by _____.

5. After practice, we treated _____ to pizza!

 With your partner, take turns talking about a group activity that you tried. Try to use reflexive pronouns.

Name _____ Date _____

The Effects of Moving

Make notes in your cause-and-effect chain as your partner tells you about a time when a friend or relative moved away.

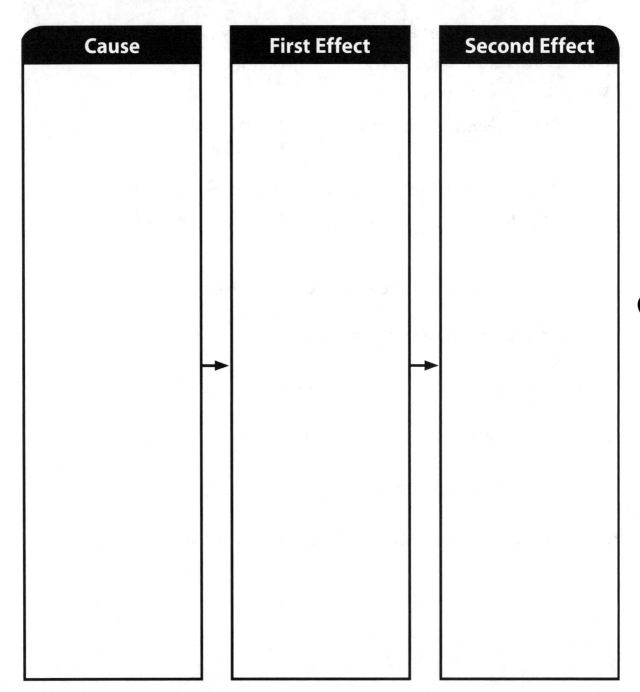

Cause	First Effect	Second Effect

 With your partner, talk about the move. Use your cause-and-effect chain to show what happened because of the move.

For use with TE p. T415a

Name _____ Date _____

Flip and Write

Directions:

1. Take turns with your partner.
   - Player 1 completes the odd-numbered sentences below.
   - Player 2 completes the even-numbered ones.

2. Players take turns flipping a coin.
   - If the coin is heads, the player completes the sentence so that it tells about things that are nearby.
   - If the coin is tails, the player completes the sentence so that it tells about things that are farther away.

3. Players check each other's sentences to see if they are correct.

4. Look at the box if you need help.

More Demonstrative Adjectives and Prounouns	
things nearby	**These** hammers are on sale. **These** are a good deal.
things father away	**Those** bags are light. You can carry **those**.

1. _____ needles are sharp. Be careful with _____.

2. _____ wheels are strong. _____ will last a long time.

3. Do you see _____ buckets? _____ will hold a lot of water.

4. _____ pans belong to a miner. _____ are very valuable to him.

5. _____ newspapers come out every day. People like to read _____.

6. Don't touch _____ pots! _____ are very hot.

7. Look at _____ gold nuggets! Whose nuggets are _____?

8. _____ boots look comfortable. You should buy _____.

Grammar: Grammar and Writing

Edit and Proofread

Choose the Editing and Proofreading Marks you need to correct the passage. Look for the following:

- correct use of possessive pronouns
- correct use of demonstrative pronouns

Editing and Proofreading Marks

∧	Add.
ℒ	Take out.

Clem pulled Millie into the store and pointed to far shelves. "See all the things on that shelf?" Clem said. "~~That~~ Those are all on sale! ∧

"Look," Clem added, showing Millie his supplies, "I have that here.

Pointing to a box of needles in the far corner, Millie said to the owner, "I need some needles. How much are these?"

He said, "This are not for sale. They are my wife's. They are his."

Ollie, a passerby, walked into the store. Holding up two water barrels, he asked, "How much can I get for that?"

"I could use a new one," Millie said. "How much are this?"

"Wait!" said the owner. "I have my own barrels for sale. You should buy one of yours."

"Forget it," snapped Millie. "I changed my mind."

"His is a fickle mind," Clem said, glancing at Millie.

Name _____ Date _____

Predict the Answer

Directions: Read each question about "The Road to Rhyolite."
Choose the best answer.

Sample

1 What is a theme of "The Road to Rhyolite"?

Ⓐ Anyone can succeed if she works hard.

Ⓑ The West is an empty and lonely place.

● Getting rich quick is a dream that often fails.

Ⓓ Ghost towns can be rebuilt.

2 Why did so many settlers head to Rhyolite, Nevada?

Ⓐ Gold had been found near Bullfrog Mountain.

Ⓑ Families traveled to Rhyolite to look for work.

Ⓒ Two railroad lines had been built in Rhyolite.

Ⓓ People stopped there on their way to Las Vegas.

3 The economy of Rhyolite changed after _____ .

Ⓐ the investors left town

Ⓑ businesses went bankrupt

Ⓒ dynamite destroyed the mines

Ⓓ the earthquake in San Francisco

 How did you use the test-taking strategy to answer the question?

Cause-and-Effect Chain

The Road to Rhyolite

Work with a partner. Complete the cause-and-effect chain below to show the major causes and effects in the play *The Road to Rhyolite*.

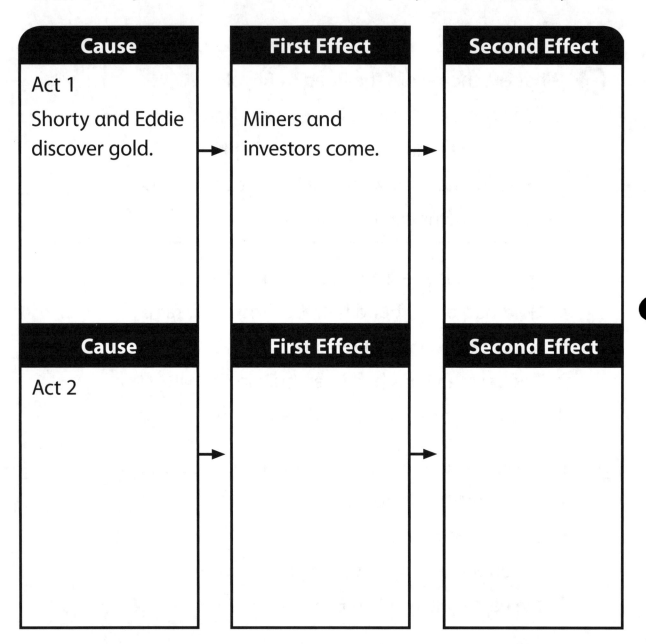

Cause	First Effect	Second Effect
Act 1 Shorty and Eddie discover gold.	Miners and investors come.	

Cause	First Effect	Second Effect
Act 2		

 Talk with a partner about other effects you may have observed in the play. Then retell the play to each other.

Fluency Practice

The Road to Rhyolite

Use this passage to practice reading with proper expression.

AGNES [*to audience*]: Well, here I am again. I know it doesn't seem	13
possible, but two years have passed since I saw you last, and things	26
are changing in Rhyolite.	30
[*Enter miners:* DOYLE, MARY, GISH, *and* YANG. *They look glum.*]	40
MARY [*angrily*]: The mines are drying up and so am I!	51
YANG: There is hardly any gold left in the ground.	61
GISH: There's only dirt and rocks and dirty socks.	70
DOYLE [*sadly*]: Looks like the good times are gone.	79
[*Enter* NEWSBOY *carrying newspapers.*]	83
NEWSBOY: Rhyolite businesses going bankrupt! Read all about it!	92
[AGNES *grabs a newspaper and reads it. Exit* NEWSBOY.]	101

From The Road to Rhyolite, page 386.

Expression

| 1 | ☐ Does not read with feeling. | 3 | ☐ Reads with appropriate feeling for most content. |
| 2 | ☐ Reads with some feeling, but does not match content. | 4 | ☐ Reads with appropriate feeling for all content. |

Accuracy and Rate Formula
Use the formula to measure a reader's accuracy and rate while reading aloud.

$$\underline{\hspace{3cm}} \quad - \quad \underline{\hspace{3cm}} \quad = \quad \underline{\hspace{3cm}}$$

| words attempted in one minute | number of errors | words correct per minute (wcpm) |

Grammar: Reteach

Party Time

Grammar Rules Pronouns

A **possessive pronoun** tells who or what owns something. A possessive pronoun agrees with its **antecedent**.	<u>My friends and I</u> have an idea. The idea is **ours**. <u>Matt</u> has decorations. The decorations are **his**.
A **demonstrative pronoun** points out or stands for a noun without naming it. • **This** and **these** stand for things nearby. • **That** and **those** stand for things far away.	**This** is my favorite CD. **These** are good chips. **That** is my game on the shelf. **Those** are puzzles over there.

Read the first sentence. Use the correct pronoun to complete the second sentence.

1. The party was Matt and Cierra's idea. The idea was _____.

2. The house next door is Sal's. _____ is where the party is.

3. Here are some games. _____ are the games I want to take.

4. I saw cookies in the kitchen. Are _____ for the party?

5. Bess has bags for everything. The bags are _____.

   With a partner, describe items in the classroom. Use possessive and demonstrative pronouns.

Grammar: Game

Indefinite Pronoun Race

Directions:

1. Play with a partner. Put your marker on START.

2. Flip a coin. Move one space for heads. Move two spaces for tails.

3. Read the word in the space.
   - If it is an indefinite pronoun, use it in an oral sentence. If your partner agrees that your sentence is correct, take another turn.
   - If the word is not an indefinite pronoun or your sentence was incorrect, your partner takes a turn.

4. The first player to reach the FINISH wins.

START	something	everybody	his	their
				you

yours	either	ours	everyone	no one
anything				
neither	this	each	nothing	anybody
				its

ours	anyone	someone	those	everything
somebody				
that	one	they	nobody	FINISH

Grammar: Game

Sort It!

Directions:

1. Players take turns writing a pronoun from the word bank into a box in the correct column of the chart until all of the pronouns are in the chart.

2. Player 1 chooses a column entry, reads the pronoun in it, and uses the pronoun in an oral sentence.

3. The other players decide whether the pronoun and the verb in the sentence agree. If they agree, Player 1 writes his or her initials in the box.

4. Player 2 and Player 3 take their turns until initials fill the chart.

5. The player with the most boxes at the end is the winner.

both	few	most
many	all	several
all	none	any

Infinite pronouns that are always plural	Infinite pronouns that can be singular or plural
_____	_____
_____	_____
_____	_____
_____	_____
	_____

Name _____ Date _____

Compare Genres

	Narrative Poem	Play
Setting		
Structure and Organization Use these words to tell about the organization and structure of the selections: • acts and scenes • dialogue • plot • rhyme • verses		

 In your opinion, which selection told the more powerful story about Rhyolite? Use your chart to help you explain your opinion.

Grammar: Different Kinds of Pronouns

All Aboard!

Grammar Rules Different Kinds of Pronouns

1. Possessive pronouns **mine**, **yours**, **his**, **hers**, **its**, **ours**, and **theirs** show who owns something and what is owned.

   We found some pickaxes. Are they <u>yours</u>?

2. Demonstrative pronouns **this**, **that**, **these**, and **those** tell about specific people, places, animals, or things without naming them.

   <u>These</u> belong to Shortie and <u>those</u> belong to Gish.

3. Indefinite pronouns **everyone**, **somebody**, **all**, **anybody**, and **anything** do not tell about specific people or things.

   <u>Anybody</u> can dig for gold in Rhyolite.

Complete each sentence with a possessive, an indefinite, or a demonstrative pronoun.

The train captain shouted, "All aboard _____! _____
(indefinite)   (demonstrative)

is the last train out of Rhyolite. We don't want to leave _____
(indefinite)

behind."

Mr. Young anxiously asked his wife, "Do you have your ticket?

_____ is in my pocket. Do the children have _____? We
(possessive)   (possessive)

must hurry to catch _____!"
(demonstrative)

Write three new sentences, each using a different kind of pronoun. Share your sentences with a partner.

Mark-Up Reading

The False Glitter of Gold by Helene Mercury

[**SETTING** *a dark, narrow canyon in the Superstition Mountains, 1868*]

JACOB WALTZ: Superstition sure is a fine name for these foothills—how easily people believe any ole rumor, overstatement, or lie! [*to* FRITZ] Bark once, buddy, if you agree that's the doggone truth.

FRITZ [*looking up at* WALTZ *and wagging his tail*]: Woof!

JACOB WALTZ [*bending over to open a chest and pull out a scroll*]: Truth is, rumors of riches brought me nothing but headaches and heartbreak—now, Fritz, if you agree, just yipyap your yes.

FRITZ [*looking up at* WALTZ *and pricking up his ears*]: Yipyap!

JACOB WALTZ: So listen to the message I'm leaving for the world. [*opens scroll and and recites in a singsong voice*] Never believe all you're told: all that glitters sure isn't gold; a legend of gold makes a terrific story, but most find neither riches nor glory. [*pauses; then with a satisfied look*] Fritz, how about howling if that isn't the most commonsense, logical, and levelheaded message I ever wrote?

[FRITZ *looks up at* WALTZ *and lets out a long howl.*]

JACOB WALTZ [*drops the scroll in the chest, then pulls a small gold nugget from his pocket*]: I guess I'll just add this, too. It is the only one I ever found. Maybe now I'll be rid of this terrible gold fever!

[WALTZ *puts the nugget in the chest and then buries the chest.*]

Name _____   Date _____

Discovering Treasure by Laura Jenkins

SCENE 1

[**SETTING** *It is the year 2012. Jasper (12 years old) and Eleanora (Jasper's younger sister) are staring at a chest they just uncovered near the Superstition Mountains in Goldfield, Arizona.*]

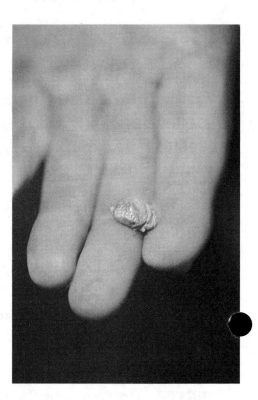

JASPER [*excitedly*]: Wow, here we are in the middle of nowhere and we find this! Could this really be the chest Jacob Waltz left behind?

ELEANORA [*inspecting the chest*]: Well if it is, then it probably contains the map to the Lost Dutchman Mine, and you know what that means. ...

JASPER [*rubbing his hands together*]: We could soon be filthy rich!

ELEANORA: And famous! I can see the headline now: "Brother and Sister Find Waltz's Lost Loot, Buy Everything Their Hearts Desire!"

JASPER: And we'll be on the news! [*holding an imaginary microphone to* ELEANORA]: Miss Eleanora, what will you do with all that gold?

ELEANORA: I'll give the first zillion to charity. With the next zillion, I'll buy a pony farm. I'll use the next zillion to fly to the moon—

JASPER [*interrupting*]: Let's go get some tools and get this thing open. I have a feeling that superstition finally just turned into reality!

[ELEANORA *and* JASPER *exit.*]

Mark-Up Reading

Discovering Treasure (continued)

SCENE 2

JASPER [*pushing a prybar beneath the lid of the chest*]: One, two… three!

[*The chest breaks open.* JASPER *and* ELEANORA *both gasp.*]

ELEANORA [*with disbelief as she grabs a lone gold nugget and examines it*]: Well, there *is* gold … but just one small nugget! [*pauses and looks into the chest again*] Hey, what are those papers there?

JASPER [*removing a few faded pieces of paper and looking at them*]: They must be what's left of the map to the Lost Dutchman Mine. I can't read a word!

ELEANORA [*looking at the papers, then collapsing*]: Oh, Jasper, we've failed! We'll never be able to find the way to the Lost Dutchman Mine now. There'll be no riches, no fame, no zillions of dollars—

JASPER [*interrupting*]: Wait, Eleanora, maybe we haven't failed entirely. I mean, we didn't find the mine, but maybe we've struck a different kind of gold, the gold of discovering a piece of history.

ELEANORA [*rolling her eyes*]: Ugh. You sound like my history teacher.

JASPER [*knowingly*]: Seriously! I mean, people have been looking for the Lost Dutchman Mine for decades. Many people don't even think it exists. Now we have found evidence that it may be real, after all. [*pauses*] Hey, we could contact the newspaper about this.

ELEANORA: Really? Do you think? [*brightening*] I can see the headline now: "Brother and Sister Find Clue to History's Great Puzzle"!

[*Light on the scene fades out.*]

Mark-Up Reading

The False Glitter of Gold Theme Chart

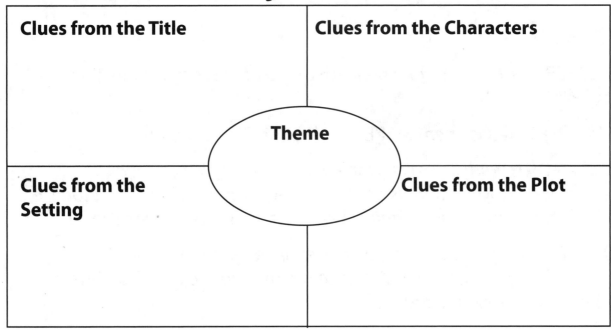

Clues from the Title	Clues from the Characters
Clues from the Setting	Theme	Clues from the Plot

Discovering Treasure Theme Chart

Clues from the Title	Clues from the Characters
Clues from the Setting	Theme	Clues from the Plot

Grammar: Grammar and Writing

Edit and Proofread

Choose the Editing and Proofreading Marks you need to correct the passage. Look for the following:

- correct use of possessive, demonstrative, and indefinite pronouns
- the use of the correct verb with indefinite pronouns

Editing and Proofreading Marks

∧	Add.
℘	Take out.

I am planning a trip to see a ghost town of Bodie, California. ~~Those~~ That would be such a cool trip. Visiting Bodie is a dream of ours.

Bodie was a typical gold-rush boom town. Now nobody live there. It is a state historical site.

Many of the travel guides says that Bodie is the country's best-preserved ghost town. It is kept in a state of "arrested decay." Those means that everything are just as it was when the town was abandoned.

Some says that there is a Bodie curse. According to park rules, nothing—not even an old nail—may be removed from the park. The curse says that anyone who take anything have bad luck. No one know if the curse is real, but it stops people from taking things.

Will I get to visit Bodie? I hope to some day!

Grammar: Reteach

Is Everyone Ready?

Grammar Rules Pronouns

Indefinite pronouns are not specific. Some are

- singular, such as **everyone**, **someone**, and **no one**

- plural, such as **both, few, many**, and **several**

- singular or plural, such as **all, many, most**, and **some** to match <u>**a noun or pronoun**</u> that follows the indefinite pronoun.

Everyone tries to dress quickly.

Many of my socks are missing.

Some of my <u>uniform</u> is dirty.

Some of <u>us</u> forget our uniforms.

Complete each sentence with the correct pronoun.

1. _____ of us dress in time for the game.
(Several / Everyone)

2. _____ shouts "Let's go!"
(Some / Someone)

3. _____ of us race out the door.
(All / Anybody)

4. _____ lines up on the field.
(Everyone / Few)

5. _____ of the players are sure we'll win!
(No one / Most)

 Use pronouns to tell a partner about different items in the classroom.

Name _____ Date _____

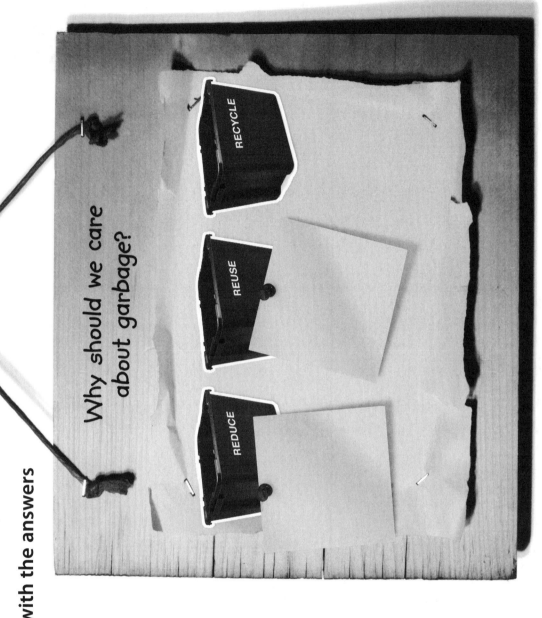

Talking About Trash

Make a concept map with the answers
to the Big Question:
Why should we care
about garbage?

Why should we care
about garbage?

RECYCLE

REUSE

REDUCE

Name _____ Date _____

Author's Viewpoint

Viewpoint	Evidence	Action Needed

 Share your ideas with another pair and listen to their ideas. If their ideas are different, see if you can agree on new, better ideas.

PM7.2 **Unit 7** | Talking About Trash

Grammar: Game

Opposite Adverbs Bingo

Directions:

1. Cut out the cards at the bottom of the page and stack them facedown.

2. Take turns picking the top card and matching it with its opposite in the grid.

3. Use each adverb in a sentence to modify a verb.

4. If your partner agrees that both of your sentences are correct, write your initials on the card. Then place the card over its opposite on the board. If either of your sentences is incorrect, return the card to the bottom of the pile.

5. The winner is the first player to have five cards in a row.

well	late	thinly	kindly	politely
first	straight	high	happily	suddenly
loudly	warmly	**FREE**	nervously	quietly
often	always	dishonestly	quickly	completely
tightly	wisely	correctly	heavily	recklessly

rudely	poorly	crookedly	calmly	foolishly	thickly
partially	low	coldly	wrongly	sadly	loosely
noisily	honestly	cautiously	seldom	slowly	never
early	lightly	softly	meanly	last	gradually

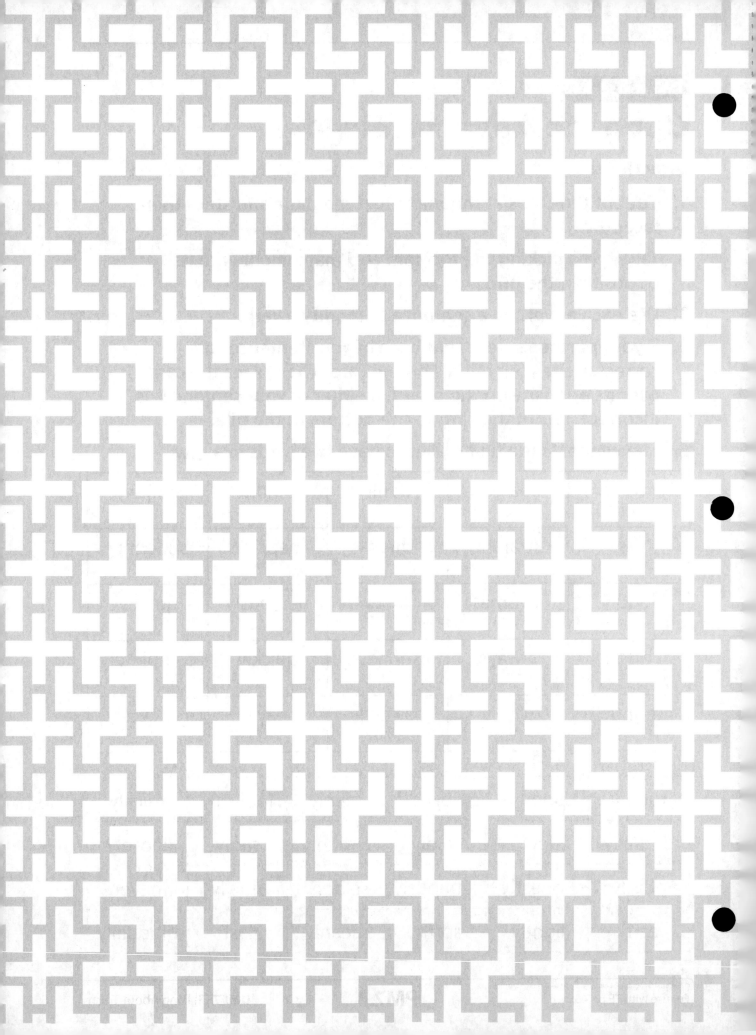

Grammar: Grammar and Writing

Edit and Proofread

Choose the Editing and Proofreading Marks you need to correct the passage. Look for the following:

- correct use of adverbs
- correct spelling of adverbs

Editing and Proofreading Marks

∧	Add.
ℒ	Take out.

The United States annual produces more garbage than any other

country. Other countries clear produce less trash. People in other

countries buy less frequent and reuse and recycle more.

We students are right concerned about the garbage problem.

But we are real lucky. Nowly we have the chance to make an

unbelievable big contribution to reducing waste. And it starts with a

zero-waste lunch.

Don't bring lunch in a paper bag with everything wrapped

separate in plastic bags. Instead, you can easy pack your lunch in a

reusable box or bag. And you can simple use washable containers

and cloth napkins that you can take home and wash routine. Forget

those juice boxes and plastic drink bottles complete. You can put

your drinks into reusable bottles instead.

Test-Taking Strategy Practice

Read All Choices

Directions: Read each question about "The World of Waste." Choose the best answer.

Sample

1 Which of the items listed below lasts the longest in a landfill?

   Ⓐ tin cans

   Ⓑ wool socks

   Ⓒ banana peels

   ● plastic bottles

2 Which country produces the most trash per person each day?

   Ⓐ United States

   Ⓑ Sri Lanka

   Ⓒ Ghana

   Ⓓ Japan

3 An earth-friendly shopper looks for products that _____ .

   Ⓐ can be used in more than one way

   Ⓑ last for a short time

   Ⓒ have thick packaging

   Ⓓ have the best commercials

 How did you use the test-taking strategy to answer the question?

Name _____ Date _____

"The World of Waste"

Viewpoint	Evidence	Action Needed
Garbage can be good.		

 Use your chart to retell the author's viewpoint and evidence to a partner. Work with your partner to find additional kinds of evidence the author uses to support her viewpoint. Add them to the evidence column.

Fluency Practice

"The World of Waste"

Use this passage to practice reading with proper intonation.

Americans win first prize! We produce more garbage than any	10
other country in the world. Look at the graphic at the right. It shows	24
about how much trash each person produces in one day, in different	36
countries. Compared with people in the United States, people in other	47
countries produce less trash. How is this possible? They buy fewer	58
things, and reuse and recycle more of them.	66
Some countries even encourage people to recycle. In	74
Switzerland, for example, people have to pay for every bag of garbage	86
they want taken away, but recyclable garbage is taken away for free.	98
Now that's a good reason to recycle!	105

From "The World of Waste", page 470

Intonation

1 ☐ Does not change pitch.   3 ☐ Changes pitch to match some of the content.

2 ☐ Changes pitch, but does not match content.   4 ☐ Changes pitch to match all of the content.

Accuracy and Rate Formula
Use the formula to measure a reader's accuracy and rate while reading aloud.

$$\frac{}{\substack{\text{words attempted} \\ \text{in one minute}}} - \frac{}{\text{number of errors}} = \frac{}{\substack{\text{words correct per minute} \\ \text{(wcpm)}}}$$

Name _____ Date _____

Grammar: Reteach

At the Movies

Grammar Rules Adverbs

An **adverb** tells more about a <u>verb</u>. It tells *how,* ***where, when, how often***, or ***how much***.	The friends **often** <u>go</u> to the movies. They **carefully** <u>choose</u> a movie to see.
An **adverb** can modify an **adjective** or another **adverb**.	They are **really curious** about "Mars Needs Kids." The movie starts **very soon**.

Read each sentence. Underline the adverb. Write what the adverb tells and which word it modifies.

1. The friends buy tickets outside the theater. _____

2. They find their seats quickly. _____

3. The movie always starts on time. _____

4. The movie is really funny. _____

5. The friends talk later about their favorite parts. _____

 With your partner, take turns describing something you did with a friend or relative. Use sentences with adverbs.

Grammar: Game

Sentence Scramble

Directions:

1. Unscramble the words in each row of puzzle boxes to make an adverb clause.

2. Find the sentence below that makes sense with each adverb clause. Write the clause on the line to complete the sentence.

3. Capitalize the first word in each sentence, and use a comma after an adverb clause at the beginning of a sentence.

4. Trade papers with a partner. Check each other's sentences to see if they are correct.

try	to	I	although	recycle
there	a	is	whenever	rainstorm	big
biodegrades	because	slowly	so	plastic
products	plastic	buy	they	before	any
built	when	boat	recycled	plastic	David	from	a

1. Trash washes up onto the shore _____

   _____.

2. _____

   it can stay in a landfill for hundreds of years.

3. People need to think carefully _____

   _____.

4. _____

   it can be difficult.

5. _____

   people didn't understand his choice of materials.

Grammar: Game

Spin and Expand

Directions:

1. Take turns spinning the spinner to go to a space. Read the adverb clause. Use the clause to write a sentence.

2. If your partner agrees that the sentence is correct, give yourself a point.

3. Play until both of you have spun four times. Who has more points?

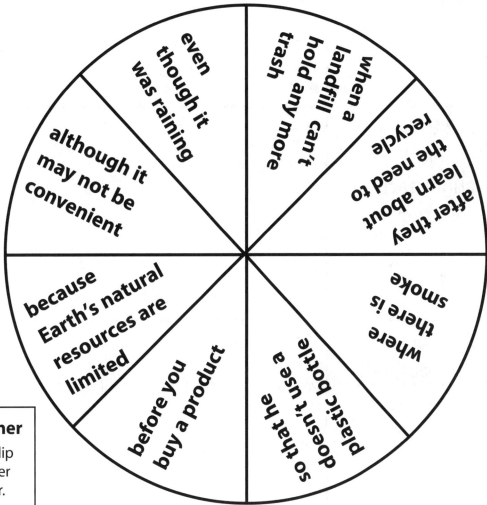

Make a Spinner

1. Put a paper clip over the center of the spinner.
2. Secure the paper clip with a pencil tip.
3. Spin the paper clip to select an adverb clause.

Authors' Purposes Chart

Compare Authors' Purposes

	"The World of Waste"	"Message in a Bottle"
Tell the author's main purpose for each selection.		
List three conclusions about each selection.		
Say how well each author's purpose was achieved.		

 Think of a book you like. Tell a partner what the author's purpose was for writing and how you know.

Grammar: Adverbs

Describe It Better

Grammar Rules Adverbs

1. Use an adverb to describe a verb.
2. Use an adverb to tell how often something happens.
3. Use an adverb to describe an adjective or another adverb.

Directions:

Add an adverb from the list below to tell more about an adverb, adjective, or verb in each sentence. Write the new sentence.

very   weekly   carefully   always

1. Some communities are creative about recycling.

_____

2. People collect cans and take them for recycling.

_____

3. They clean the empty cans so they are safe.

_____

4. Some people bring their own bags when they shop.

_____

 Tell a partner another creative way to recycle. Use at least one adverb in your sentence.

Name _____ Date _____

PLASTIC:
Some Clear, Hard Facts
by Boris Maletski

Plastic is everywhere in our "throwaway" world—from soda bottles to sandwich bags and from razors to diapers. Plastics make life easier, but many pose a huge threat to the environment because they don't decay like natural materials. Luckily, there are solutions to this problem. People can reduce plastic use. Manufacturers can also change the way plastics are made.

▲ Plastics are convenient but can pose a huge threat to the environment.

A common type of plastic waste is water bottles. Thirty billion plastic water bottles were sold in the U.S. in 2005. The problem is that about 80% of them were thrown out after one use. Some made their way to the ocean, harming or even killing sea birds and mammals. One way to help solve this problem is to buy reusable water bottles and repeatedly refill them. States can also change the law. What if all stores charged a ten-cent deposit fee for each plastic bottle sold? Then people would have a strong incentive to return their empty bottles for recycling—getting their deposit money back!

Another common type of plastic waste is bags. By one estimate, Americans use 60,000 plastic bags every five seconds! One way to use fewer plastic bags is to reuse the bags. People could also try purchasing reusable cloth or canvas bags to take shopping. Some cities, like Seattle, Washington, have even banned single-use plastic bags entirely.

PLASTIC:
Some Clear, Hard Facts

(continued)

Scientists are also working to highlight the problem of plastic waste. They have learned that chemicals used to make plastic don't break down for hundreds of years. Their evidence also shows that some of the harmful chemicals used to make plastic can enter the water supply.

▲ Biodegradable plastics decay in days instead of centuries.

Luckily, scientists also offer solutions. One idea is to make plastic using biodegradable materials that will quickly and easily break down in a landfill or in the environment. Some people are embracing the idea and trying new ways to make plastic using corn, soy, and even chicken feathers! Such solutions can be a win-win for the environment and farmers. For example, chicken farmers throw away four billion tons of chicken feathers yearly. What if those feathers could be put to a new use?

Across the country and throughout the world, people are working to help solve the problem of plastic. When it comes to plastic, the facts are clear: less plastic means a cleaner environment.

Name _____ Date _____

○ ○ ○

◀ ▶ ▾ | C | ✕ | ⌂ | http://www.ngreach.com | ○ | 🔍

EARTH DAY Every Day

| Home | Garbage & Pollution | Fact Sheets | **How You Can Help** |

▼ **How You Can Help**
- **Reduce**
- Reuse
- Recycle

▶ Saving Water

▶ Green Schools

Reduce

Reduce means to use less. Using less creates less waste.

Every year, Americans use billions of plastic shopping bags. This creates hundreds of thousands of tons of waste. What if people stop using plastic bags and instead bring their own reusable bags when they shop? This would reduce the amount of plastic waste considerably!

People also use billions of disposable plastic cups and utensils every year. This waste could circle the equator hundreds of times! Instead, of wasting all those plastic knives, forks, and cups, people could use utensils that can be washed and reused. The result would be many fewer items going into the trash.

Reuse

Reuse means to use something over again or to find another use for it. Reusing a product keeps it out of the trash.

People can purchase reusable plastic products like storage containers rather than items that can be used only once. Reducing the amount of plastics people use only once also reduces the amount of plastic products made.

Disposable plastics can be reused in a number of creative ways. For example, some businesses sell woven plastic products like hats, rugs, and even jewelry. What ideas do you have for reusing plastic and keeping it out of the trash?

Name _____ Date _____

Recycle

Recycle means to convert products back into raw materials to make other products. For example, some plastics can be melted down and molded into new products like carpet fiber and textiles. Recycling saves energy and reduces the amount of waste we dump in landfills.

Most plastic does not biodegrade. It breaks into small pieces that litter the soil and the water and never go away. Instead, recycling plastic keeps the Earth clean and allows plastic to be used again in a different product.

Plastics are labeled with a recycling number. Plastics labeled with the numbers 1 or 2 can be made into lots of new products. Plastics with higher numbers are tougher to recycle, so people should try to buy only plastics that can be recycled.

If people follow the three "Rs," someday we may never have to worry about plastic waste again!

Integrate Information: _____

_____

_____

_____

_____

_____

Grammar: Grammar and Writing

Edit and Proofread

Choose the Editing and Proofreading Marks you need to correct the passage. Look for the following:

- correct use of adverbs and adverb clauses.
- correct punctuation
- correct spelling of adverbs

Editing and Proofreading Marks

∧	Add.
℘	Take out.
⌒∧	Move to here.
∧̣	Add comma.
⊙	Add period.

I want to be environmental responsible. Therefore, I am taking a no-plastic pledge.

Even though it is extreme inconvenient I take my lunch to school in a lunch box. I pack my sandwiches in reusable containers, which I take home at night. When I have leftovers I take them home. They go immediate into the compost bin.

Equal inconvenient is carrying my own cloth shopping bag. But I do it glad for the sake of the environment. When you shop have you ever counted the number of plastic bags you get? My mom did, and the number is outrageous high. Plastic bags are already banned in many countries. I real hope our country will ban them soon, too.

Grammar: Reteach

A Run in the Park

Grammar Rules Adverb Clauses

An **adverb clause** is a dependent clause that acts like an adverb. Adverb clauses tell **why, where, when**, or **how often**.	As often as I can, I go to the park.
A **subordinating conjunction**, such as **as, when, where, before, because**, or **although** signals an adverb clause.	Before I go, I do my chores.
Use commas for **adverb clauses** at the beginning or in the middle of a sentence.	After I do chores, I start to run. I run a mile, when I can, then turn back.

Read each sentence. Underline the adverb clause. Circle the subordinating conjunction.

1. Before I start, I stretch my legs.

2. When I arrive at the park, James is waiting for me.

3. We run together because we both like company.

4. We stop for a while, where the fountain is, to catch our breath.

5. As we often do, we run two miles.

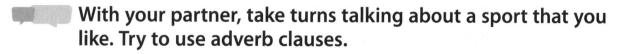 **With your partner, take turns talking about a sport that you like. Try to use adverb clauses.**

Name _____ Date _____

A Goal-and-Outcome Story

Somebody (character(s))	Wanted (goal)	But (obstacle(s))	So (outcome)

 Work with a partner to tell about goals, obstacles, and outcomes in a story you have read recently.

Adverb Puzzle

Directions:

1. Fill in the missing irregular comparison adverbs in the puzzle pieces.

2. Use the words in the puzzle pieces to complete the sentences below. Use each word only once. Be careful! Work in pencil. The sentences do not always go from weakest to strongest!

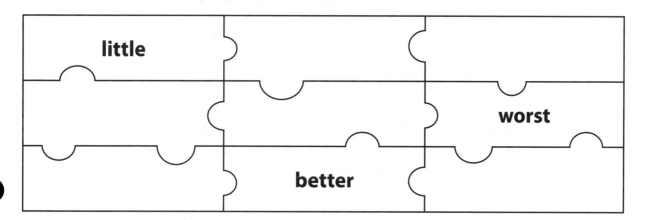

1. The toddlers—Chin, Phil, and Lina—speak _____.

2. Of the three toddlers, Lina speaks _____.

3. Chin speaks _____ than Phil.

4. Joelle plays soccer _____ than any player I know.

5. Ben practices every day, so he plays soccer _____.

6. Jackie wants to play soccer _____ _____ of all the players on the team.

7. Tula practiced her handwriting because she wrote _____.

8. The teacher said Tula wrote _____ than any of her classmates.

9. But Tula knew someone who wrote _____ _____ of all.

Edit and Proofread

Choose the Editing and Proofreading Marks you need to correct the passage. Look for the following:

- correct spelling of adverbs
- correct use of regular and irregular comparison adverbs

Editing and Proofreading Marks

∧	Add.
✎	Take out.

    Len sat on his stoop and looked around. People had littered the

street fast∧than ever. "People are littering often than before," Len

more said sadly. "It may be hard than ever to get them to stop, but

I'm going to do something about it."

    So Len met with his friends Caitlin and Mike. When Len described

his plan, Caitlin said enthusiastically, "I'm in!" And Mike said even

more enthusiasticallier than Caitlin, "Me, too!" So the three friends

worked tirelesslier on their plan than they had ever worked before.

    Caitlin wanted people to litter the least. So she made signs that

stated CAN IT TO SAVE THE PLANET. Mike was shy, so he didn't work

better with people. He composted leftovers and showed others how

to do it clear than a lesson would have. Len's pet peeve was gum, so

he set up NO STICK zones. Anyone who tried to spit out gum was

properlier corrected.

Test-Taking Strategy Practice

Read All Choices

Directions: Read each question about "Where I Live."
Choose the best answer.

Sample

1 Which sentence is the best main idea for "Where I Live?"

Ⓐ Garbage collectors take care of all litter in a
   neighborhood.

Ⓑ Landfills are the best ways to get rid of our waste.

● Every citizen is responsible for his or her neighborhood.

Ⓓ Most food is sold in disposable wrappers.

2 Elena gets upset when _____ .

Ⓐ she sees people litter

Ⓑ her mother asks her to run errands

Ⓒ she has to do homework

Ⓓ she can't buy what she wants

3 What does Ricky do with his gum wrapper?

Ⓐ He throws it in the recycling bin.

Ⓑ He gives it to Elena.

Ⓒ He puts it in his pocket.

Ⓓ He throws it onto the sidewalk.

 **How did you use the test-taking strategy to answer
the question?**

Name _____ Date _____

"Where I Live"

Somebody (character(s))	Wanted (goal)	But (obstacle(s))	So (outcome)
Elena			

 Work with a partner. Tell what clues you used to figure out Elena's goals and obstacles. Then work together to talk about Ricky's goals and obstacles. Add them to your chart.

PM7.23

Fluency Practice

"Where I Live"

Intonation is the rise and fall in the pitch or tone of your voice as you read aloud. Use this passage to practice reading with proper intonation.

"Hey," I call to Ricky, who is now by himself. Where did Pablo	13
What's-His-Name go? Maybe his mother called him—mothers are	24
always yelling from open windows, " *¡Venaca!* It's time to eat!"	34
Ricky, whose shoelaces are undone, joins me, the marbles	43
clicking in his pocket with each step.	50
You're probably thinking, do I LIKE Ricky? No. He's smaller	60
than me, only seven years old, and likes marbles and his army men.	73
Also, if he were to show you his knees, you would see that they have	88
scabs the color of bacon. I don't have scabs, and unlike Ricky, who	101
always has mocos sliding out of his nostrils, I almost never catch colds. And if I	117
do, I use tissue and dispose of it properly.	126

From "Where I Live," page 507

Intonation

[1] ☐ Changes voice to match all the content	[3] ☐ Changes voice, but it does not match content
[2] ☐ Changes voice to match some of the content	[4] ☐ Does not change voice

Accuracy and Rate Formula
Use the formula to measure a reader's accuracy and rate while reading aloud.

$$\underline{\hspace{3cm}} - \underline{\hspace{3cm}} = \underline{\hspace{3cm}}$$

words attempted in one minute	number of errors	words correct per minute (wcpm)

Grammar: Reteach

Hiking Up the Mountain

Grammar Rules Adverbs

To compare two actions, add **-er** to many adverbs. Use **more** or **less** for adverbs ending in **-ly**.	This mountain reaches **higher** than that one. That path winds **more steeply** than the road.
To compare three or more actions, add **-est** to many adverbs. Use **the most** or **the least** for adverbs ending in **-ly**.	This mountain reaches the **highest** of all the mountains. Max hikes **the most eagerly** of all his friends.
Some adverbs are irregular: **well, better, best** **badly, worse, worst**	I hike **well**. She hikes **better** than I do. Ana feels **badly**. Lara feels **worse**.

Write the correct word to complete the sentence.

1. Max hikes _____ than I hike. (better, best)

2. I climb _____ than he does. (high, higher)

3. Ana walks the _____ of all. (most slowly, slowliest)

4. Max climbs the _____ . (more fast, fastest)

5. This hike is _____ than the last one! (worst, worse)

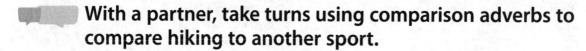 **With a partner, take turns using comparison adverbs to compare hiking to another sport.**

Grammar: Game

Preposition Clues

Directions:

1. **Choose a player to begin. Then, take turns in a clockwise fashion.**

2. **Toss a coin onto a square and read the preposition it lands on. If the preposition shows . . .**

   - *location*, use it to describe the location of an object in the school. ("This object is *outside* the classroom.")

   - *direction*, use it to describe the movement of an object. ("This object moves *around* the sun.")

   - *time*, use it to describe an event. ("This event happens *during* lunch.")

3. **The other players guess what the object, movement, or event is. Guessers can use other prepositions to ask more questions. (e.g. Is it *on* the playground? Is it *beyond* Earth?)**

4. **Play continues until each player has had three turns.**

over	before	behind	during
inside	to	up	around
in front of	under	after	below
out	down	outside	from

Name _____   Date _____

Grammar: Game

Recycle the Prepositions

Directions:

1. **Play with a partner. Player 1 reads sentence 1, underlines the prepositional phrase, and circles the preposition. If player 2 agrees, player 1 scores 1 point.**

2. **Player 2 "recycles" the prepositional phrase in sentence 1 by writing it in the correct box at the bottom of the page. If player 1 agrees, player 2 scores 1 point.**

3. **Players switch roles and repeat until there are no more sentences.**

---

1. Streams and creeks are great places for kids.

2. Over the years, many have become polluted.

3. Drive toward the hills, and you may find a polluted stream.

4. You and your friends can adopt a stream in need of help.

5. Take a trash bag and wear heavy gloves on your hands.

6. Fill the bag and take the trash to a recycling center.

7. Get some adults to plant trees along the stream banks.

8. In no time, the stream will be beautiful again.

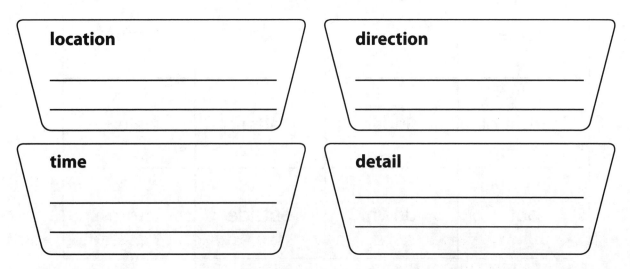

location	direction
_____	_____
_____	_____

time	detail
_____	_____
_____	_____

Character Description Chart

Compare Characters

Character	What the Character Does	What This Shows About the Character
Elena	She tells people to pick up their litter. She gets angry when she sees waste on the street. She dreams about choosing an ice-cream flavor. She dreams about a flower box with beautiful flowers.	Elena is bossy.
Sarah		

 Talk with a partner. Compare two other story characters you know about.

Grammar: Prepositional Phrases

Ricky's Story

Grammar Rules Prepositional Phrases

1. Use prepositional phrases to show location:

   Ricky played <u>near Elena's apartment</u>.

2. Use prepositional phrases to show direction:

   Elena and Ricky headed <u>down the street</u>.

3. Use prepositional phrases to show time:

   <u>After school</u>, Ricky plays marbles with his cousin Pablo.

4. Use prepositional phrases to give details:

   Elena wrote a report <u>about recycling</u>.

Write prepositional phrases.

My name is Ricky, and I live _____ as Elena. I

play marbles _____ after school every day. One day

_____, Elena asked me to go with her _____ to buy

eggs and milk. When we saw the ice cream treats _____,

we dreamed _____. When Elena paid for the eggs

and milk, Mr. Asmara gave us some gum. Elena yelled at me when I

threw the gum wrapper _____. She taught me

an important lesson: Don't litter!

 Tell a partner about places where you can find litter. Use prepositional phrases in your sentences.

Mark-Up Reading

Where Will We Run To? by X. J. Kennedy

Where will we run to
When the moon's
Polluted in its turn

And the sun sits
With its wheels blocked
In the used star lot?

▲ Factory smoke rises towards the moon.

Structure: _____
_____
_____

Imagery: _____
_____
_____
_____

Visual: _____
_____
_____
_____

Mark-Up Reading

Secretary Bird by Alice Schertle

Take a letter:

Say that
the ancient trees are falling.
Say that
the whale's song grows faint.
Say the passenger pigeon is gone.
The great auk is gone.
The rhino, the mountain gorilla,
almost gone...

▲ Secretary Bird

Structure: _____
_____
_____
_____

Imagery: _____
_____
_____
_____

Visual: _____
_____
_____
_____

Mark-Up Reading

Secretary Bird (continued)

Dip your quill

in the sludge

along the river,

in the soot

from the smokestack,

in the poisoned lake,

in the burning rain.

Dip it in the blood of the great blue whale.

take a letter, bird:

to whom it may

concern

▲ Secretary Bird

Structure: _____

_____

_____

_____

_____

_____

Imagery: _____

_____

_____

_____

_____

Mark-Up Reading

Landscape by Eve Merriam

What will you find at the edge of the world?

A footprint,

a feather,

desert sand swirled?

A tree of ice,

a rain of stars,

or a junkyard of cars?

What will there be at the rim of the earth?

A mollusk,

a mammal,

a new creature's birth?

Eternal sunrise,

immortal sleep,

or cars piled up in a rusty heap?

Structure: _____

_____

Imagery: _____

_____

Visual: _____

Grammar: Grammar and Writing

Edit and Proofread

Choose the Editing and Proofreading Marks you need to correct the passage. Look for the following:

- correct use of prepositions
- correct use of prepositional phrases

Editing and Proofreading Marks

∧	Add.
ℐ	Take out.

Did you know that Americans use one-third more water ~~while~~ ∧ during the summer than the rest the year? Why? It's because we water our lawns. The United States has millions acres of lawns. Watering that much grass takes billion of gallons water every week. With that much water every person under the world could take a shower four days along a row.

To prevent wasting water, people should water their lawns only early for the morning or late on night. Doing this prevents the water by evaporating, or drying up, in the heat by the day. People who use sprinklers need to be sure that the water falls only before the lawn and not with the sidewalk or driveway. Nothing grows there, so that is just another waste water.

Grammar: Reteach
Walking the Dog

Grammar Rules Prepositions

A **preposition** links a noun or pronoun to other words in a sentence. Prepositions show location, time, or direction.	I walk the dog **on** the sidewalk. I can walk the dog **until** dinner. I walk the dog **across** the park. I walk the dog **for** an hour.
A <u>prepositional phrase</u> always begins with a **preposition** and ends with a noun or pronoun.	I walk the dog **to** <u>the supermarket</u>.

Read the sentences below. Circle the preposition and underline the prepositional phrase.

1. I walked my dog, Sandy, to the lake.

2. She jumped into the water!

3. I called her and raced around the lake.

4. Finally, she bounced up the path.

5. We ran home after the fun.

 With a partner, talk about a time you went for a walk or hike. Use prepositional phrases to describe what you did.

How can one idea change your future?

Unit Concept Map

One Idea

Make a concept map with the answers to the Big Question:
How can one idea change your future?

For use with TE p. T533

PM8.1

Name _____   Date _____

Tell Steps in a Process

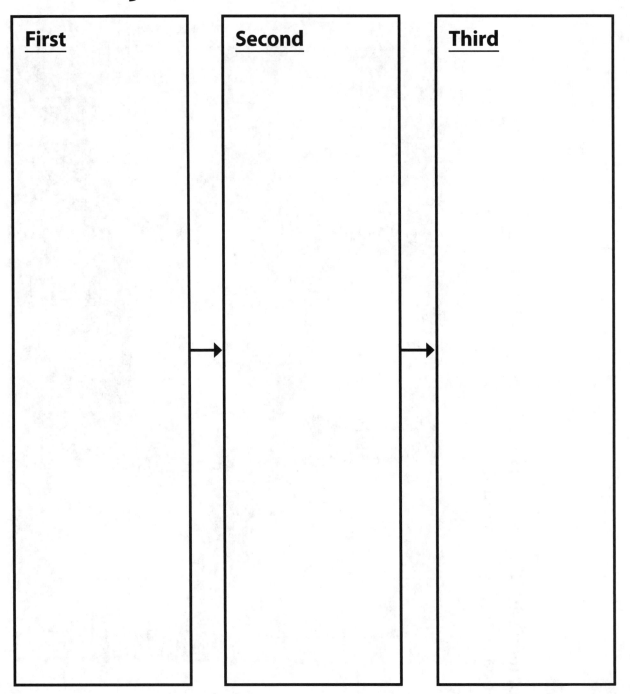

| First | Second | Third |

Use a sequence chain to tell a partner the steps that you would take to start a business. Use the words *first*, *second*, and *third* to explain the steps in an order that makes sense.

Grammar: Game

Spin a Tense

Directions:

1. Play with a partner. Take turns.

2. Spin the paper clip. Read the verb.

3. Use the past-progressive form of the verb to write a sentence.

4. If your partner agrees that you have used the past-progressive form of the verb correctly and that you have spelled the main verb correctly, score one point.

5. Then your partner takes a turn.

6. After all the verbs have been used once, count your points. The partner with more points wins.

Make a Spinner

1. Place one loop of a paper clip over the center of the circle.

2. Push a sharp pencil through the loop and the paper.

3. Spin the paper clip around the pencil.

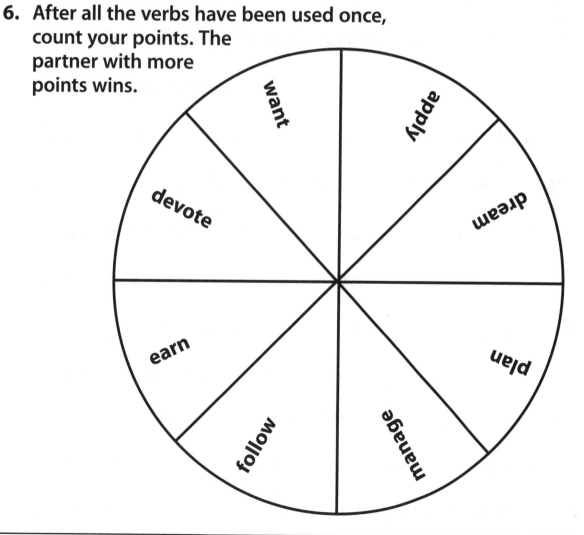

Grammar: Grammar and Writing

Edit and Proofread

Choose the Editing and Proofreading Marks you need to correct the passage. Look for the following:

- correct use of past-progressive tense
- correct use of regular and irregular verbs in past-perfect tense

Editing and Proofreading Marks

∧	Add.
ℰ	Take out.

Dallas looked at her business plan. She ~~works~~ on it for a long time. *(had worked added above)* But she knew there was still something she forgetting. She showed the plan to her dad—to see if he could tell what were missing.

Mr. Weisel examined Dallas's list of equipment. He saw that she had listed almost everything she was going to need for her dog-walking business. But he spotted something Dallas had not saw.

Mr. Weisel reminded Dallas that the city recently had passing a "pooper-scooper" law, so Dallas would have to clean up after the dogs.

Dallas groaned. She was neglected to include biodegradable bags on her list of start-up expenses. She had knowed about this law, but hadn't remember. She had hoping she was finished adding up expenses, but she added them up again anyway. Now the list felt complete, but her costs had double!

Skip and Return to Questions

Directions: Read each question about "Starting Your Own Business." Choose the best answer.

Sample

1 An entrepreneur is someone who _____.

   Ⓐ makes and stores goods

   Ⓑ takes and uses an income

   Ⓒ has a supply of products

   ● starts and manages a business

2 What is *income*?

   Ⓐ money you take in

   Ⓑ a business plan

   Ⓒ money you spend

   Ⓓ profit you make

Directions: Read the question. Then write your answer in the space.

3 What is one step you need to take before starting a business?

_____

_____

Directions: Complete the sentence by writing the correct word on the blank.

4 Entrepreneurs must raise their own start-up _____.

   How did you use the test-taking strategy to answer the question?

Name _____ Date _____

"Starting Your Own Business"

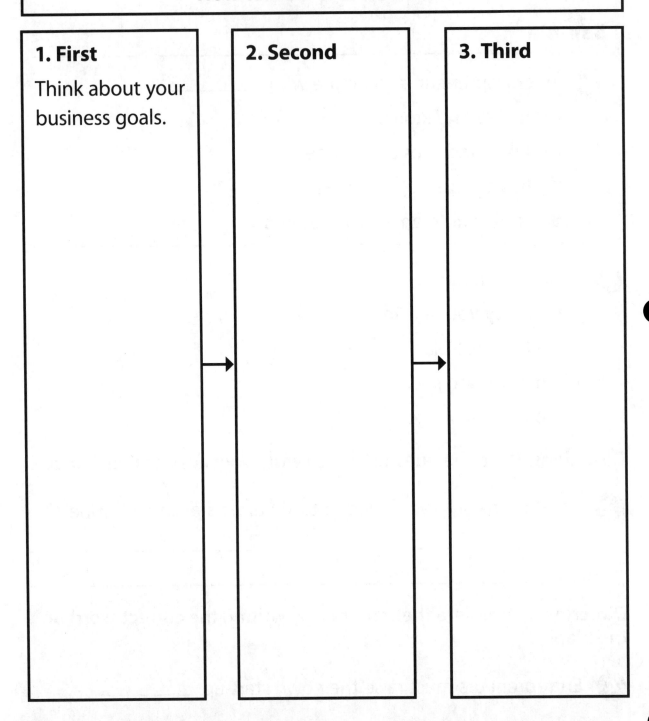

How to Plan Your Business

1. First

Think about your business goals.

2. Second

3. Third

 Use your organizer to explain the procedure to a partner.

"Starting Your Own Business"

Use this passage to practice reading with proper phrasing.

Have you ever dreamed of having lots of money of your own?	12
Then you should think about starting a business. Every year, thousands	23
of kids start businesses. They earn extra money to spend or to save.	36
Some kids use their business earnings to pay for trips, lessons, or	48
for college later on. Kids do more than just babysit or mow laws.	61
Many kids have found ways to make their businesses different	71
and special.	73
People who start and manage their own businesses are	82
entrepreneurs. Entrepreneurs are good planners and organizers.	89
Before starting a business, an entrepreneur finds a need and thinks	100
about how to fill it. Starting a business isn't always easy, but it's usually	114
challenging and fun.	117

From "Starting Your Own Business," pages 542-543

Phrasing

1 ☐ Rarely pauses while reading the text.   3 ☐ Frequently pauses at appropriate points in the text.

2 ☐ Occasionally pauses while reading the text.   4 ☐ Consistently pauses at all appropriate points in the text.

Accuracy and Rate Formula

Use the formula to measure a reader's accuracy and rate while reading aloud.

$$\underline{\hspace{3cm}} - \underline{\hspace{3cm}} = \underline{\hspace{3cm}}$$

words attempted   number of errors   words correct per minute
in one minute   (wcpm)

Grammar: Reteach

Living on a Budget

Grammar Rules Past-Tense Verbs

A **past-progressive** verb tells about an action that was happening over a period of time in the past. • Use **was** or **were** with a main verb ending in **-ing**.	Mia's parents **were planning** a budget.
The **past-perfect** tense tells about an action that was completed before another action in the past. • For **regular** verbs, use **had** and a main verb ending in **-ed**. • For **irregular verbs**, use **had** and a **special form** of the main verb.	Before they <u>made</u> it, they **had shopped** carelessly. Mia **had** never **thought** about money until she <u>saw</u> the budget.

Proofread the sentences. Correct the errors in verb usage.

1. Mia were wondering about how she could help her family.

2. She realized that she spent money carelessly in the past.

3. In the new budget, her parents was cutting her allowance.

4. She never earned money, but she wanted to help.

5. Before summer started, she had make a plan for business.

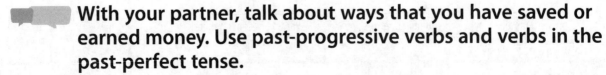 **With your partner, talk about ways that you have saved or earned money. Use past-progressive verbs and verbs in the past-perfect tense.**

Make Them Past Tense

Directions:

1. Play with a partner.

2. Use a paper clip, eraser, or other small object as a game marker and place it on START.

3. Flip a coin to move. Heads = 1 space; tails = 2 spaces.

4. Read the verb on the space where you land, and write its past-tense form.

5. If your partner agrees that you spelled the past-tense form correctly, stay where you are. If not, go back one space.

6. Take turns. The first player to reach FINISH is the winner.

START	dry	analyze	stop	surprise
				slam
imagine	grab	classify	divide	rely
trim				
amuse	occupy	snap	observe	FINISH

Grammar: Game

Irregular Bingo

Directions:

1. Play with a group. Each player writes a verb from the word bank on each square of the Bingo grid in any order.

2. Select a caller to read the words in the word bank in random order.

3. Find the verb on your bingo card as the caller reads it. Write its past-tense form in the square.

4. If the group agrees that you wrote the past-tense form correctly, cover the square with a marker. If not, erase your writing.

5. Play until a player gets five markers in a row and calls "Bingo."

do	see	throw	speak	bring	know
write	eat	ride	grow	fly	give
get	run	wear	fall	think	go
lose	begin	say	sit	take	sing

___	___	___	___	___
___	___	___	___	___
___	___	**FREE**	___	___
___	___	___	___	___
___	___	___	___	___

Name _____ Date _____

Compare Procedures

Steps in "Starting Your Own Business"	Steps Kayla Legare Used
1. Plan your business	✓
2.	
3.	
4.	
5.	
6.	
7.	

 Take turns with a partner. Share one way Kayla could have completed one of the steps that isn't checked.

Grammar: Regular and Irregular Past-Tense Verbs

Kayla's Menus

Grammar Rules Regular / Irregular Past-Tense Verbs

1. For most verbs, add *-ed* to form the past tense (ordered).

2. Add just *-d* to verbs that end in silent *e* (baked).

3. Double the final consonant for verbs that end in vowel + consonant (fanned).

4. Change *y* to *i* and add *-ed* for verbs that end with consonant + *y* (tried).

5. Remember special past-tense forms for *is, are, do, go, take*.

Write the past tense of the verb.

Kayla _____ special software to make menus for blind and
           (use)

visually impaired people. She _____ her business with her
                                    (plan)

uncle. He _____ interested and wanted to help her. They
              (is)

_____ to talk to restaurant owners. Kayla _____ that no
     (go)   (worry)

one would buy her menus. She and her uncle _____ happy
                                                  (are)

that restaurants bought the menus.

 Listen when a partner tells you a verb. Tell the past tense of the verb. Tell the spelling rules to make the past tense.

Name _____ Date _____

Making Bucks *by* Washing Pups by Mai Nguyen

▲ Washing dogs can be fun and profitable.

Do you love dogs? If so, consider starting a dog washing business. To be successful, begin with a plan that includes where you will wash the dogs. Then think about the materials you will need, such as shampoo, hoses, towels, and a tub. Also list who you think your customers might be.

Next, do the numbers. Add up all your costs and decide how many customers you might get each week. Figure out what you should charge to begin making a profit within three months.

Show your detailed plan to your parent(s) and explain your goals. Then, if they give permission, get (and take!) their advice.

Text Structure: _____

Maddie's FishFlops by Amit Sinha

▲ Maddie displays some of her flip-flop designs.

Because Maddie Robinson loved sketching sea creatures at the beach, it was no surprise when, one day, she sketched a flip-flop design with sea animals on it. She named it a FishFlop.

Maddie's father saw the business possibilities right away. He registered for the FishFlops.com domain name and talked with a lawyer about getting a trademark.

Since Maddie and her father wanted people to see the product, they began making samples and taking them to trade shows. Customers began to flip for FishFlops, and the business grew!

Text Structure: _____

Mark-Up Reading

From Super Idea to SuperJam
by Edgar Wilson

EDINBURGH, SCOTLAND—It all started with a super idea. When he was only fourteen, Fraser Doherty's grandmother taught him to make her delicious jam using her secret recipe. Fraser decided to go into business selling it.

▲ Fraser Doherty

Fraser began his operation on a shoestring, making jam in his parents' kitchen and selling it to his neighbors and at local farmers' markets. Soon demand skyrocketed.

It was only logical to expand his business. Analyzing the market, he saw an opportunity for healthier, sugar-free jams. Eliminating one of the two main ingredients in his jam was not a piece of cake. And to top it off, he had to figure out how to keep his expenses down so that he could continue to make a reasonable profit. But Fraser finally found a way to sweeten his jam with only fruit juice, making it more popular than ever.

After that, Fraser needed to greatly increase production. He got a loan and rented a factory to help him produce his SuperJam. On the first day his SuperJam was sold in stores, the supermarket sold more jam in that one day than it usually sold in an entire month.

SuperJam is now sold in several supermarket chains across the United Kingdom and Ireland and is a huge success! Looking back, Fraser thinks anyone can accomplish what he did with determination and imagination. He has proven that one simple idea can become a reality!

Text Structure: _____

Name _____ Date _____

Diego's Awesome Salsa
by Karen Chu

SACRAMENTO, CALIFORNIA—Have you heard the saying "When it rains, it pours"? If not, just ask ten-year-old entrepreneur Diego Bartolome. He can tell you what it means.

Diego's troubles began, oddly, with his success. A few years ago, Diego started a business selling jars of homemade salsa at a local bakery. His salsa was a hit. Before he knew it, Diego had $1,000 in earnings!

Diego's business grew, and soon, a local television program, *Good Day Sacramento,* invited him to appear. Sounds like a young entrepreneur's dream, right? Not so fast!

▲ Diego's salsa is full of fresh tomato taste.

An inspector from the state Department of Health saw Diego on TV. He noticed that Diego's salsa jars weren't labeled properly and was concerned Diego wasn't keeping them at the proper temperature. He contacted Diego and his mom to inform them that they needed to purchase a health permit, which had a starting cost of $350 a year.

The permit was just the tip of the iceberg. Diego also needed health inspections, new labels and jars, and a business license to help him comply with the law. All of these things cost money—something that, in Diego's household, was in short supply.

Luckily, the solution to Diego's financial problems was right under his nose—salsa. Diego continued working hard, and sales of his salsa went through the roof. He is now selling up to four cases a week, and has paid all the necessary fees to keep his business within the law. Diego has also learned how important it is to stick with it in business and life. Not a bad lesson for someone only ten years old!

Text Structure: _____

Name _____ Date _____

Compare Text Structures

"Making Bucks by Washing Pups"	Both	"Maddie's FishFlops"

"From Super Idea to SuperJam"	Both	"Diego's Awesome Salsa"

Grammar: Grammar and Writing

Edit and Proofread

Choose the Editing and Proofreading Marks you need to correct the passage. Look for the following:

- correct spelling of past-tense verb forms
- correct use of irregular past-tense verbs

Editing and Proofreading Marks

∧	Add.
ℐ	Take out.

    Even when blind people could order from a Braille menu, they still

had
~~haved~~ a problem: paying the bill. There's no way for a blind person
  ∧

to tell the difference between a $1 bill and a $100 bill.

    Many other countries have paper money that helps blind people.

Years ago, the European Union changes their paper money to help

the blind. It make the paper money with foil textures to distinguish

the bills. Australia create a similar raised-texture system. Canada

putted raised dots on its currency.

    In 2008, a federal court rules that U.S. currency discriminates

against the blind. The U.S. Treasury Department fighted the court

ruling for years. The Department sayed that changing the size of U.S.

paper money would cost billions of dollars. But now the Department

has a mobile phone application to help blind people with U.S. bills.

Grammar: Reteach

Trip to the Moon

Grammar Rules Past-Tense Verbs

The **past tense** form of a regular verb ends with **-ed**.	The rocket blast<u>ed</u> into the sky.
• For verbs that end in silent **e**, drop the **e** before adding **-ed**.	We hop<u>ed</u> to land on the moon.
• For verbs that end in one vowel + one consonant, double the final consonant before adding **-ed**.	Finally, the spacecraft drop<u>ped</u> to the surface.
• For verbs that end in a consonant and **y**, change **y** to **i** before adding **-ed**.	Valeria cr<u>ied</u> with happiness when we landed.
The **irregular past tense** does not add **-ed**.	I <u>brought</u> a camera. I <u>took</u> pictures.

Circle the past-tense verb of the underlined present-tense verb.

The surface of the moon <u>is</u> (was, ised) dusty. Ted <u>try</u> (tryd, tried) to put moon rocks in his bag. We enjoyed the view of Earth. I <u>dig</u> (dug, digged) a hole. Valeria <u>unroll</u> (unroled, unrolled) the flag. Ted <u>place</u> (placied, placed) the flag in the hole. The flag <u>show</u> (showed, showd) that we had been there.

 Pick two past-tense verbs from above and write new sentences. Read them to a partner.

Name _____ Date _____

Elements of Fiction

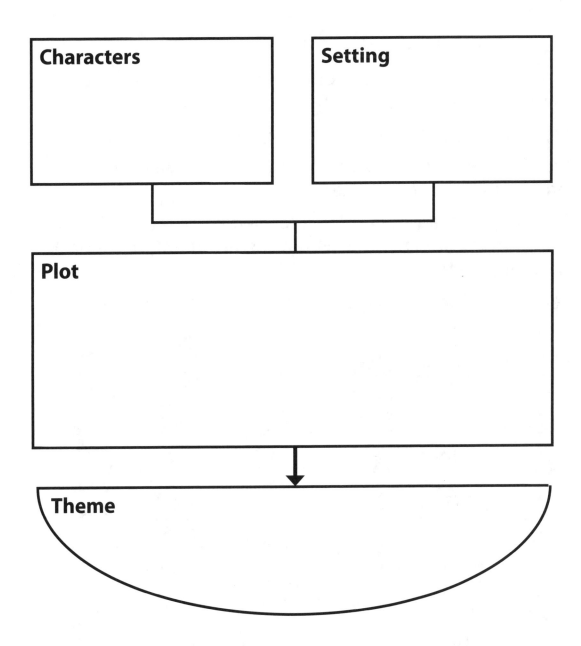

Characters

Setting

Plot

Theme

💬 Retell the story to a partner using your story map.

Grammar: Game

Climb to the Future Progressive

Directions:

1. Play with a partner.

2. Use a paper clip, eraser, or other small object as a game marker and place it on START.

3. Flip a coin to move. Heads = 1 rung; tails = 2 rungs.

4. Read the verb on the rung where you land. Use its future-progressive form in a sentence.

5. If your partner agrees that you formed and used the future progressive correctly, stay where you are. If not, move back down one rung.

6. Take turns. The first player to reach END is the winner.

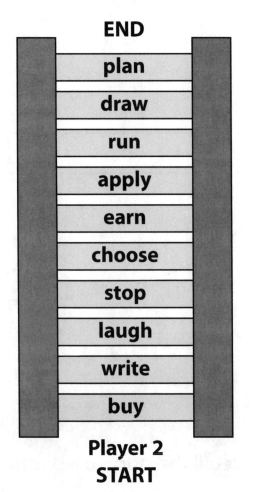

END	**END**
run	plan
buy	draw
plan	run
write	apply
draw	earn
apply	choose
laugh	stop
stop	laugh
earn	write
choose	buy
Player 1 **START**	**Player 2** **START**

Grammar: Grammar and Writing

Edit and Proofread

Choose the Editing and Proofreading Marks you need to correct the passage. Look for the following:

- correct use of past, past perfect, and future-progressive verbs
- correct form of irregular verbs

Editing and Proofreading Marks

∧	Add.
⸲	Take out.

    Before Europeans arrived in western Africa, Ghana had ~~being~~ been part
of an ancient trade route. By 1472, Portuguese had arrive ashore

and had saw that the local people wore gold jewelry. That had

attracted people from Portugal and other European countries. The

area became known as the Gold Coast. After Europeans had maked

contact, locals were greatly impacted. Europeans wanted to protect

their trade interests, so they construct forts and castles. Originally,

trade had center on the gold, which was available in the area.

    After the British gained control of the area, it makes Ghana

a British colony. In the 1900s, inhabitants of the Gold Coast

start to take control of their country. They finally will be gaining

independence on March 6, 1957. Today, Ghana is one of the leading

countries in Africa. Hopefully, Ghana will be enjoy a bright future.

Test-Taking Strategy Practice

Skip and Return to Questions

Directions: Read each question about "One Hen." Choose the best answer.

Sample

> **1** What does *organization* mean?
>
> Ⓐ something you are unfamiliar with
>
> Ⓑ a person who starts a business
>
> ● a business or other official group
>
> Ⓓ money received from a bank

2 How does Kojo use the money he saved in the first year of selling eggs?

Ⓐ buys toys to play with

Ⓑ pays his mother back

Ⓒ goes to the market

Ⓓ goes back to school

Directions: Read the question. Then write your answer in the space provided.

3 Kojo's grandson asks where all of the eggs go. Why does Kojo respond, "To your future, my child"?

_____

_____

_____

 How did you use the test-taking strategy to answer the question?

Name _____ Date _____

"One Hen"

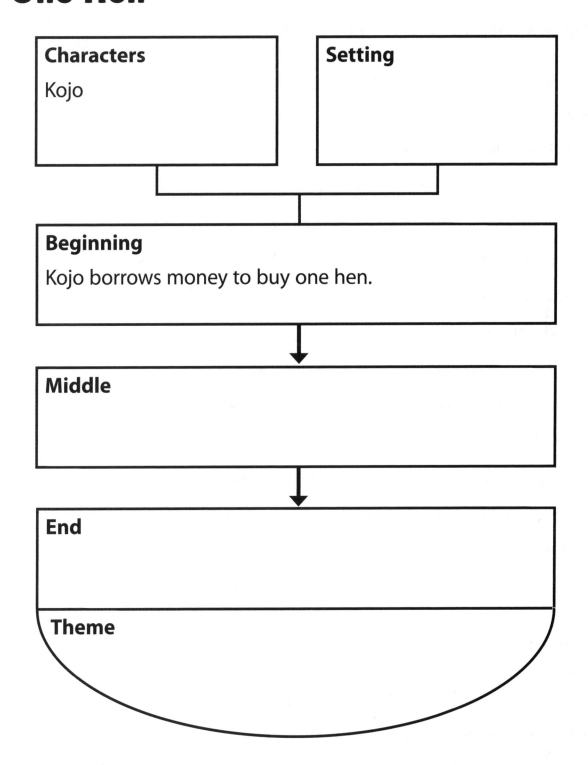

Characters

Kojo

Setting

Beginning

Kojo borrows money to buy one hen.

Middle

End

Theme

💬 **Use your story map to retell the story to a partner. Tell how you decided what the theme was.**

"One Hen"

Use this passage to practice reading with proper expression.

Before long, many people are working on Kojo's farm. Men   10

feed the chickens and clean the coops. Women collect the eggs and   22

pack them in boxes. Other workers drive the eggs to markets.   33

The workers have families. One hundred and twenty people   42

depend on the wages from Kojo's farm. Families like the Odonkors   53

have enough food to eat and money for their children's school fees.   65

Ma Odonkor can buy medicine when her daughter Adika falls ill. Pa   77

Odonkor can rebuild the walls of their mud home with cinderblocks.   88

The workers on Kojo's farm can even afford livestock of their   99

own. Some families buy a goat, others a sheep, and some start with   112

one brown hen.   115

Kojo's farm is now the largest in Ghana. One day, Kojo hears a   128

knock at the door. Adika Odonkor, all grown up, is there. She greets   141

Kojo and holds out a small sack of coins.   150

From "One Hen," pages 586-587

Expression

1 ☐ Does not read with feeling.

2 ☐ Reads with some feeling, but does not match content.

3 ☐ Reads with appropriate feeling for most content.

4 ☐ Reads with appropriate feeling for all content.

Accuracy and Rate Formula

Use the formula to measure a reader's accuracy and rate while reading aloud.

$$\frac{\text{_____} - \text{_____} = \text{_____}}{}$$

| words attempted in one minute | − | number of errors | = | words correct per minute (wcpm) |

Grammar: Reteach

Working Together

Grammar Rules Past and Future Verb Tenses

For events in the past, be sure to use the correct verb tense.	had known I ~~knew~~ Becca for years before we ∧started this project. were working While we ∧~~had worked~~ together, I learned to appreciate Becca's good ideas.
For an action that will be happening over a period of time in the future, use a **future-progressive verb.** Use **will be** with a main verb ending in **-ing**.	Becca and I **will be planning** a new project next week.

Proofread the sentences. Correct errors in verb usage.

1. Next summer, Jasmine and I will be attend science camp.

2. We will planning and building a robot together.

3. Last year we both had gone to an outdoor adventure camp.

4. As we was hiking and camping together, we had learned to trust each other.

5. We be learning many more things together next summer.

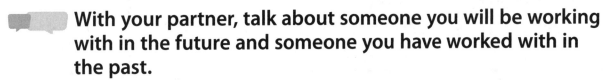 **With your partner, talk about someone you will be working with in the future and someone you have worked with in the past.**

Name _____ Date _____

Race for the Future

Directions:

1. Play with a partner.

2. Use a paper clip, eraser, or other small object as a game marker and place it on START.

3. Flip a coin to move. Heads = 1 space; tails = 2 spaces.

4. Read the verb on the space where you land, and write it in the future-perfect tense.

5. If your partner agrees that you formed the future perfect correctly, stay where you are. If not, go back one space.

6. Take turns. The first player to reach FINISH is the winner.

START	dry	hid	stop	choose
				grab
imagine	grip	knock	run	rely
write				
take	occupy	eat	observe	FINISH

Grammar: Game

Follow the Future

Directions:

1. Play with a partner.

2. Use a paper clip, eraser, or other small object as a game marker and place it on START.

3. Roll a die to move in any direction.

4. Follow the directions in the space you land on.

5. If your partner agrees that you formed and used the future perfect correctly, stay where you are. If not, you lose a turn.

6. Take turns. The first player to reach END is the winner.

START	Roll again.	Form the future perfect of *eat*.	Go back one space.	Use the future perfect of *wait* in a sentence.
Use the future perfect of *break* in a sentence.	Form the future perfect of *throw*.	Go ahead one space.	Ask a question with the future perfect of *sit*.	Roll again.
Go back two spaces.	Lose a turn.	Form the future perfect of *break*.	Go ahead one space.	Use the future perfect of *finish* in a sentence.
Roll again.	Form the future perfect of *talk*.	Go back one space.	Use the future perfect of *apply* in a sentence.	Ask a question with the future perfect of *win*.
Lose a turn.	Form the future perfect of *run*.	Use the future perfect of *pick* in a sentence.	Go back two spaces.	END

Comparison Chart

Compare Texts

	"Another Way of Doing Business"	"One Hen"
Name the businesses.		Hens and eggs
Who started it?		Kojo
Where did the start-up costs come from?	A small-business loan	
Name the start-up materials.		
Do you think it will continue to be successful? Why?		

 Talk with a partner about ways businesses can help people.

Name _____   Date _____

Ana's Dream

Grammar Rules Future-Tense Verbs

1. Use *will* + *main verb* to tell about the future.

   I <u>will go</u> to the store in the morning. She <u>will go</u> with me.

2. Use *to be* + *going to* + *main verb* to tell about the future.

   I <u>am going to buy</u> firewood. She <u>is going to buy</u> tools.

Write future-tense verbs. Use both rules.

Ana was tired of her job. Her dream was to be her own boss.

Ana thought to herself, "Tomorrow, I _____ to the
(Rule 1: go)

bank and ask for a loan. I _____ my own business. I
(Rule 2: start)

_____ a learning center for young children.
(Rule 1: open)

At first, the banker did not want to give Ana a loan, but Ana

said, "I _____ hard, and you _____ that I
(Rule 1: work)   (Rule 1: find)

_____ my loan quickly. The banker knew that Ana would
(Rule 2: repay)

keep her word. "You _____ your loan," he said. "Together,
(Rule 1: get)

we _____ sure your business succeeds."
(Rule 2: make)

Tell a partner what you would like to do for work when you are older. Use both rules in your sentences.

Name _____ Date _____

SMALL LOANS
Make Big Differences
by Olivia Wattly

Matt Flannery has always been an "idea" person. He loves to spend time thinking up new ideas. Back in 2003, Flannery worked as a software developer for a large company. Still, what he really wanted to do was to become a business entrepreneur. Little did he know that his goal was about to become a reality.

Flannery and his fiancée, Jessica Jackley, went to hear Dr. Mohammad Yunus speak at Jessica's college. Yunus's words inspired them. Within a year, they had created Kiva, an organization that gives small business loans to people all over the world.

Relationship: _____
_____
_____
_____

The way Kiva works is simple. First, entrepreneurs apply for a loan through Kiva's Web site. Next, lenders from around the world visit the site and choose which businesses they want to provide with a loan. Unlike Yunus' bank program, Kiva's program depends on individual donations. Once borrowers receive their loans, they can then slowly repay these loans over time as their businesses grow and succeed.

Relationship: _____
_____
_____

Mark-Up Reading

SMALL LOANS
Make Big Differences (continued)

Elizabeth Omalla, a widow with seven children, was one of the first people affected by Kiva. Omalla's goal was to grow her business. However, her fish-selling business made only a small profit, and Omalla needed that money to support her family. As a result, she could not afford a bus ticket to travel to the lake where the fish she sold were caught. Instead, she had to buy fish from a middleman and resell them, so she made less money.

Relationship: _____
_____
_____
_____
_____

Omalla applied for a loan through Kiva, and information about her business went on Kiva's Web site. Lenders read her story, and eventually provided Omalla with a $500 loan. As a result of the loan, Elizabeth was able to travel to the lake and buy fish herself. Because she no longer had to use a middleman, Omalla could buy more fish for a lower price, and she was able to grow her business.

Omalla's story is one of thousands. All over the world, people are loaning money to entrepreneurs like Omalla, and helping them succeed. The loans may be small, but their impact is huge.

▲ Kiva has helped many women start or grow a business.

Relationship: _____
_____
_____

Grammar: Grammar and Writing

Edit and Proofread

Choose the Editing and Proofreading Marks you need to correct the passage. Look for the following:

- correct use of future-perfect tense
- correct use of future tense
- correct form of irregular verbs

Editing and Proofreading Marks

∧	Add.
ℐ	Take out.

There it was again, that question: What are you going to ~~have~~

be
~~been~~ when you grow up? That's a tough question for us eleven-year-
∧

olds. We may no longer want to be firefighters or astronauts. But we

is not willing to say, "I will help endangered species," or "I is going

to be an accountant." By the end of this week, I will have change my

mind ten times about what I want to be.

I read an article last week about choosing a career. It said to

follow your interests. Right now I'm interested in baseball. Does

that mean I am go to become a professional baseball player? What

are the chances of that? My sister is a really good dancer. Will she

grown up to be a professional ballerina? That's also doubtful.

Finding a common ground between interests and reality is go to be

tricky. Perhaps by the time I'm twenty, I will had developed realistic

interests that is going to lead to a career.

Grammar: Reteach

Saving Your Money

Grammar Rules Future Verb Tenses

A **future tense** verb tells about an action that will happen in the future. • Use **will** + a main verb. • Or, use **am/is/are** + **going to** + a main verb.	Toby **will save** part of his earnings. Toby **is going to save** part of his earnings.
The **future-perfect** tense tells about an action that will be completed <u>by a specific time in the future</u>. • For **regular** verbs, use **will have** + a main verb ending in **-ed**. • For **irregular verbs**, use **will have** and a **special form** of the main verb.	<u>By September,</u> he **will have saved** enough to buy a bike. <u>By the time summer ends,</u> he **will have made** several hundred dollars.

Write the correct form of each verb in parentheses. Use the future tense or the future-perfect tense.

1. (save) I _____ my money so that I can buy a new video game.

2. (save) By next month, I _____ enough money for the game.

3. (earn) This summer, Lacey _____ money by babysitting.

4. (buy) By August, she _____ a lot of new clothes.

5. (spend) By the time school starts, she _____ half her savings.

 With your partner, talk about ways you will save money in the future. Use verbs in the future and future-perfect tenses.